A
bounty
OF **bead**
& **wire**
BRACELETS

A bounty OF bead & wire BRACELETS

50 fun, fast JEWELRY projects

NATHALIE MORNU

LARK CRAFTS

Asheville

Editor
Nathalie Mornu

Editorial Assistant
Hannah Doyle

Art Directors
Carol Morse Barnao
Kathleen Holmes

Art Intern
Jessica Yee

Production
Kay Holmes Stafford

LARK CRAFTS

An Imprint of Sterling Publishing
387 Park Avenue South
New York, NY 10016

If you have questions or comments about
this book, please visit: larkcrafts.com

Library of Congress Cataloging-in-Publication Data

Mornu, Nathalie.
  A bounty of bead & wire bracelets : 50 fun, fast jewelry projects / Nathalie Mornu. -- 1st ed.
    p. cm.
  Includes index.
  ISBN 978-1-4547-0407-2
  1. Jewelry making. 2. Bracelets 3. Beadwork. 4. Wire jewelry. I. Title. II. Title: Bounty of bead and wire bracelets.
  TT212.M664 2012
  745.594'2--dc23

                                    2011047754

10 9 8 7 6 5 4 3 2 1

First Edition

Published by Lark Crafts
An Imprint of Sterling Publishing Co., Inc.
387 Park Avenue South, New York, NY 10016

Distributed in Canada by Sterling Publishing,
c/o Canadian Manda Group, 165 Dufferin Street
Toronto, Ontario, Canada M6K 3H6

Distributed in the United Kingdom by GMC Distribution Services,
Castle Place, 166 High Street, Lewes, East Sussex, England BN7 1XU

Distributed in Australia by Capricorn Link (Australia) Pty Ltd.,
P.O. Box 704, Windsor, NSW 2756 Australia

ISBN 13: 978-1-4547-0407-2

For information about custom editions, special sales, and premium and corporate purchases, please contact the Sterling Special Sales Department at 800-805-5489 or specialsales@sterlingpub.com.

Requests for information about desk and examination copies available to college and university professors must be submitted to academic@larkbooks.com. Our complete policy can be found at www.larkcrafts.com.

contents

22

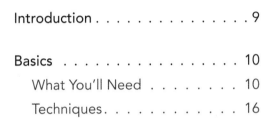

25

28

30

32

36

38

40

43

46

48

51

56

54

56

58

60

62

64

66

68

70

73

76

77

 84

80

87

90

92

96

98

100

102

103

106

108

110

99

112

114

116

118

120

122

126

128

130

132

134

137

introduction

Bracelets aren't just pretty embellishments for your wrists. These jingly accessories accent your personality—especially when you're the one who makes them. When you create your own bracelet, you choose the types of beads, colors, wires, metals, and fashions that best suit your style. With *A Bounty of Bead & Wire Bracelets*, an entire menu of exciting choices is at your disposal: I've selected 50 of the most popular bracelet projects from an array of best-selling Lark Jewelry & Beading books for you.

Just pick your favorite projects, and in no time you'll round out your wardrobe with a range of stylish cuffs, bangles, charm bracelets, and more, each with a unique aesthetic and character. For a vintage feel, try Apple Blossoms (page 110), a French-inspired charm bracelet featuring glass apples, flowers, and cabochons on a brass chain. For a well-traveled look, make Temple Gate (page 22), an exotic piece that combines Chinese porcelain, Czech glass, and Thai silver beads.

Practice coiling with Wire & Crystal (page 43), a funky cuff composed of wrapped coils and crystals suspended between a silver wire frame. Try your hand at chain mail with the very contemporary Nexus (page 36), whose clusters of interconnected jump rings enclose red carnelian beads. Test your skills for crafting simple loops and jump rings with Golden Dunes (page 70), a gorgeous bracelet made from conch shell beads, mother-of-pearl nuggets, and coin shells, all bound together with dazzling wraps of gold-filled wire.

With its 50 fun, fast projects, this book covers every imaginable style of bead and wire bracelet. Its basics section and in-depth instructions serve as your loyal guide, so you'll be able to make that bracelet you've been dying to wear, whether you're a beginner or an experienced crafter.

So forget the pricey manufactured bracelets you see in stores. You can make your own fabulous bangles, and have plenty of fun in the process!

basics

The most basic elements of drawing and painting are lines and points. It's easy to think of wire as a linear element, and beads as dots. Use these simple building blocks to become a jewelry artist and make the beautiful bracelets in this book!

WHAT YOU'LL NEED

The materials and tools described here are your essential jewelry-making kit. Where you'll really have fun is while shopping for beads and wire. If you've never worked in this medium, you're in for hours and hours of browsing—the hardest part is stopping!

Beads

Whether you hunt for them in craft stores, attend huge bead shows, or surf the Net, beads are readily available and more affordable than ever. Elegant pearls, faceted gem briolettes, Bali beads, glass donuts, drilled pebbles, resin globes—you have an incredible array of choices.

Most stores organize their beads by their material, shape, and diameter. It's kind of like taking a trip around the globe: there are shimmering Austrian crystals, glass beads lampworked in India, carved cinnabar from China, African trade beads, brightly painted beads from Peru, and that's just a start!

Sizing

Beads are measured in millimeters. In case you happen to be more accustomed to inches, photocopy the comparison chart (figure 1) and bring it along when you shop. You can buy beads individually or in strands. Most strands measure 16 inches (40.6 cm) long, with the number of beads on each strand determined by their individual sizes.

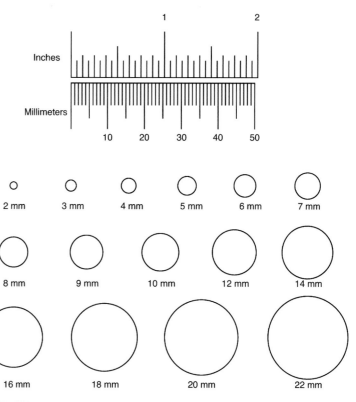

fig. 1

Holes: Orientation and Diameter

The position and size of the hole drilled in the bead, crystal, or pearl will have a huge effect on the finished piece because it determines how the bead will be attached.

A bead with a hole that runs from the top to the bottom is called length drilled. This is the most common treatment. If nothing is specified in the supply list of a project, assume you need length-drilled beads. When the hole is through the width, it's a horizontal drill. A top-drilled bead, crystal, or pearl has a hole near the top.

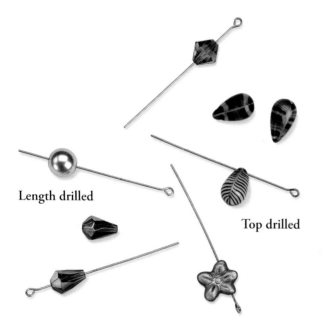

Length drilled

Top drilled

The size of a hole is an issue to consider. If your bracelet requires stronger, heavier wire, you'll need to get beads with larger holes. Furthermore, depending on the product, the hole size may not be consistent from one bead to the next. When in doubt, check that the hole size is adequate by running the wire you intend to use for your project through each bead.

Wire

Look for wire in beading stores, in jewelry supply shops, at craft retailers, and in the electrical supply and framing departments of hardware stores. Depending on the type of metal, wire is sold on spools, in prepackaged coils, by weight, and by length. (The Internet is also a vast resource for wire of every kind.)

Wire made from sterling silver or gold is a popular choice for bead and wire bracelets, but many other wire products can be used, too. Metal craft wire comes in a wide variety of colors. (Relative newcomers to this category include anodized and dyed metals, such as aluminum or niobium.) Still other kinds of wire exist: steel, brass, nickel, copper, and even platinum. These are malleable. Then there's super-springy memory wire, made from base metal or stainless steel, which can be stretched and permanently bent but will always retain its initial coiled silhouette.

Various gauges and types of wire (from top): gold wire, silver wire, and memory wire

Wire comes in a large range of sizes and shapes. Gauge is the scale of measurement that indicates the diameter of the wire—the higher the number, the finer the wire. (Memory wire is the exception to gauge measurements; it's sold in sizes to fit the wrist, neck, or finger.) The Key to Wire Gauges chart lists helpful information about wire gauges and their specifications, both metric and standard.

key to wire gauges

AWG IN.	AWG MM	GAUGE	SWG IN.	SWG MM
0.204	5.18	4	0.232	5.89
0.182	4.62	5	0.212	5.38
0.162	4.12	6	0.192	4.88
0.144	3.66	7	0.176	4.47
0.129	3.28	8	0.160	4.06
0.114	2.90	9	0.144	3.66
0.102	2.59	10	0.128	3.25
0.091	2.31	11	0.116	2.95
0.081	2.06	12	0.104	2.64
0.072	1.83	13	0.092	2.34
0.064	1.63	14	0.080	2.03
0.057	1.45	15	0.072	1.83
0.051	1.30	16	0.064	1.63
0.045	1.14	17	0.056	1.42
0.040	1.02	18	0.048	1.22
0.036	0.914	19	0.040	1.02
0.032	0.813	20	0.036	0.914
0.029	0.737	21	0.032	0.813
0.025	0.635	22	0.028	0.711
0.023	0.584	23	0.024	0.610
0.020	0.508	24	0.022	0.559
0.018	0.457	25	0.020	0.508
0.016	0.406	26	0.018	0.457

Wires of the same gauge will all feel different to work with because some metals are softer than others. As you work with it, wire stiffens a bit in a process called *work hardening*. This trait can be of benefit by adding more support to your work. If wire gets overmanipulated, however, it becomes brittle and breaks.

Silver and gold wires are made and sold in different hardnesses: dead soft, soft, and half hard. Avoid dead-soft wire; it's difficult to work with and won't retain shaping or angles. For most of these projects, the designers have recommended the appropriate wire hardness; when they haven't, use half-hard wire.

Many of the bracelets in this book are made with sterling silver wire, but wire made from an *alloy*—a blend of less expensive metals—is fine to use instead, especially for jewelry for daily wear. And if you plan to make a bracelet from very expensive wire, it's really smart to practice first with a cheap wire of similar gauge and hardness.

You can substitute gauges other than those given in the project instructions, but remember that very thin wire, though easier to shape, won't be strong enough to hold a bunch of heavy beads, while thick wire isn't going to look good when used for small-scale designs—not to mention the limitation of the size of the bead holes.

Findings

You're probably going to need more than just beads and wire to create your bracelet. Findings are that extra ingredient. They're usually made of metal and are meant to connect, finish, and embellish your design.

Clasps connect wire ends to hold the bracelet closed. There are dozens of different types. Here are some of the most common.

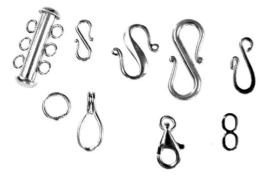

Box clasps have one half that's comprised of a hollow box. The other half is a tab that clicks into the box to lock the clasp.

Hook-and-eye clasps have one half that's shaped like a hook and the other half like a loop, or an "eye." The hook passes through the eye to secure the clasp.

Lobster-claw clasps are spring-activated clasps that are shaped like their name.

Magnetic clasps use powerful magnets to make the connection between one half of the clasp and the other. Use these only with fairly light-weight pieces, and if you have a pacemaker, don't use them at all.

Toggle clasps have one half that looks like a ring with a loop attached to it, and the other half looks like a bar. Pass the bar through the ring, and once the bar lies parallel on top of the ring, you've secured the clasp.

Bead caps fit over the tops and bottoms of beads. They're used to finish a strand of beads or as spacers between beads.

Spacers are small elements used to separate and set off the beads in a design. They can be plain or fancy.

Chain is made up of connected loops of wire. The loops can come in several forms, including round, oval, twisted, and hammered.

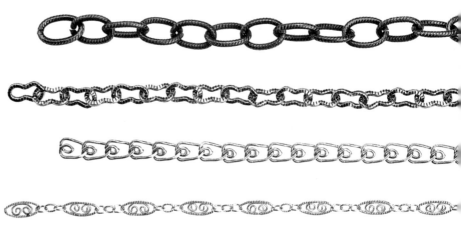

Crimp tubes and crimp beads secure the ends of beading wire to keep the beads on while providing the means for attaching a clasp or finding.

Jump rings are circular loops of wire used to connect beadwork to findings or findings to findings. They come in open and soldered-closed versions. You can find them at any beading or craft retail store in a variety of colors and metals.

Eye pins are straight pieces of wire with a simple loop at one end. They're used to make beaded links.

Head pins are used for stringing beads to make dangles. Simple head pins are composed of a straight wire with a tiny disk at one end to hold beads in place. Ball-end head pins have a ball at the end instead of a disk. There are even fancier head pins, too.

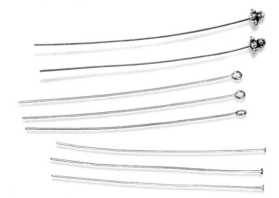

Tools

Making bead and wire bracelets requires just a few low-tech tools. Try to buy the best quality you can afford.

Pliers have either serrated or smooth surfaces on their jaws. If you're going to invest in a set of pliers, make sure they're smooth jawed. These are preferable for jewelry making because they won't scratch wire. If you want to use the serrated pliers you already have, you can wrap the jaws with surgical adhesive tape to protect your work—just be careful to avoid getting any of the adhesive on your materials.

Chain-nose pliers

Crimping pliers

Chain-nose pliers feature jaws that are flat on the inside but taper to a point on the outside. This type of pliers also comes in a bent version used for grasping hard-to-reach places.

Crimping pliers attach crimp beads and crimp tubes to beading wire. See page 19 for instructions on how to use these.

Flat-nose pliers have jaws that are flat on the inside and have a square nose.

Round-nose pliers have cylindrical jaws that taper to a very fine point.

Wire cutters have very sharp blades that come to a point. One side of the pliers leaves a V-shaped cut; the other side leaves a flat, or flush, cut.

Mandrels are any straight or tapered rod around which you wrap wire to shape it into coils. They're essential for making jump rings, the loops in closures, or uniformly sized units for links. You can buy one with various diameters (shown here) or simply use a nail, knitting needle, dowel, or any household item with a rodlike shape.

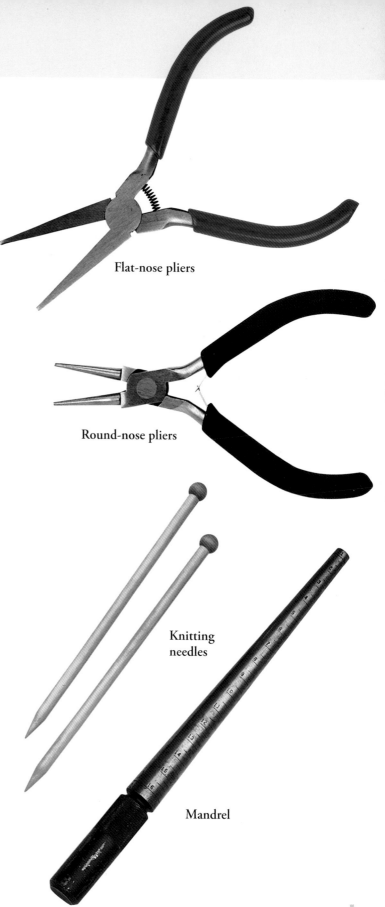

Flat-nose pliers

Round-nose pliers

Knitting needles

Mandrel

Wire cutters

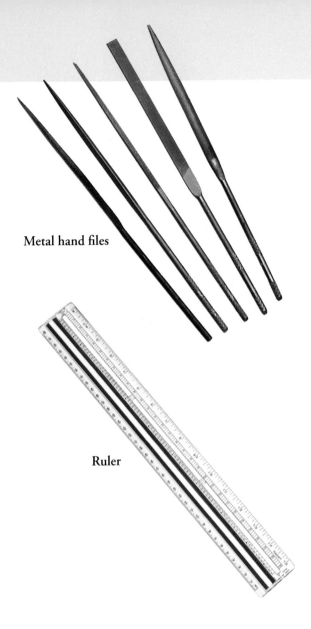

Metal hand files

Ruler

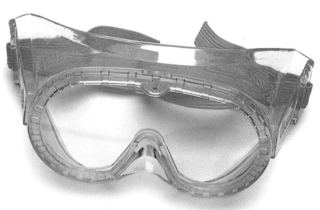

Safety glasses

Jigs are flat boards with holes drilled at regular intervals. Place pegs in the holes to bend wire around, creating perfect loops. You can purchase them commercially or make your own without too much effort.

Emery boards are for sanding wire smooth. **Metal hand files, or needle files**, have very fine teeth. They also smooth wire ends.

Tape measures and rulers will help you determine where to cut wire and chain. They're also helpful for checking bracelet lengths and bead and finding sizes. Choose one that has both standard and metric markings.

Safety glasses are important to wear when making metal jewelry because they protect your eyes from flying wire pieces.

TECHNIQUES
Study the techniques below and you'll make jewelry like a pro in no time flat.

Wirework Skills
In this section you'll learn to wrangle wire into a great bracelet design with basic wire techniques. Unless you're already familiar with them, you'll probably want to start by practicing these techniques with a piece of low-cost wire—it's not easy to straighten wire once it's bent the wrong way.

Controlling Wire
The best-looking bracelets have smooth and confident swoops, angles, and curves made from kink-free wire. Hold spooled wire in check by keeping it in a small baggie. Simply pull out wire as needed. If you're working with a coil of wire rather than a spool, wrap it with masking tape so it can't spring open in all directions.

Straightening
To keep it in good condition, wire is stored and sold in coils. Coiling wire saves space, but it's best to straighten out its curve before you begin working with it. To straighten a short length of wire, hold one end of it with chain-nose pliers. Just above the pliers, grasp the wire with a cloth or paper towel to keep your hands clean and to prevent friction burn. Squeezing your fingers slightly, pull the length of wire through them.

If the wire bends or crimps at any time, gently run your finger along it to smooth the kink, or rub the wire over the edge of a table padded with newspaper. Don't smooth a crimp too vigorously, or the wire could break. Remember, the more you shape the wire, the more it work hardens and becomes brittle.

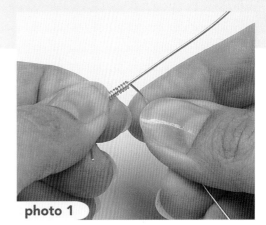

photo 1

Coiling

Coiling, or tightly wrapping, wire is used in this book primarily for attaching one wire to another and creating decorative coils. Start by grasping the mandrel—a thick wire, dowel, or knitting needle—tightly in one hand. Hold the wrapping wire with your other hand and make one wrap. Reposition your hands so you can continue to wrap the wire around the base wire, making tight revolutions (photo 1).

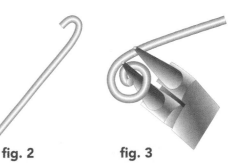

fig. 2   **fig. 3**

Spiraling

Spiraling is a great technique to add depth and embellishment to your design or even to create the focal point of your piece.

1. Use the tip of a pair of round-nose pliers to curve one end of the wire into a half-circle or hook shape about ⅛ inch (3 mm) in diameter (figure 2).

fig. 4

2. Use the very tips of the pliers to curve the end of the wire tightly into itself, as shown in figure 3, aiming to keep the shape round rather than oval. Hold the spiral in flat- or chain-nose pliers and push the loose end of the wire against the already-coiled form (figure 4); as you continue, reposition the wire in the pliers as needed.

Simple Loops

1. Use chain-nose pliers to make a 90° bend ⅜ inch (1 cm) from the end of the wire; if you're using the loop to secure a bead (as with a bead dangle), make the 90° bend right at the top of the bead, then cut the wire ⅜ inch (1 cm) from the top of the bead (photo 2).

photo 2

2. Use round-nose pliers to grasp the wire end and roll the pliers until the wire touches the 90° bend (photo 3).

photo 3

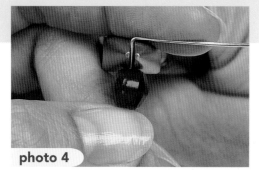

photo 4

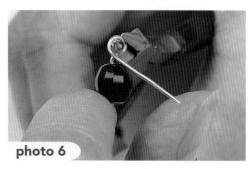

photo 5

photo 6

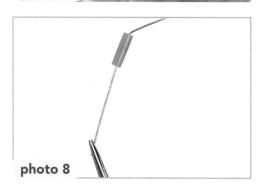

photo 7

photo 8

Wrapped Loops

1. Use chain-nose pliers to make a 90° bend in the wire 2 inches (5.1 cm) from one wire end or ¼ inch (6 mm) from the top of a bead (photo 4).

2. Using round-nose pliers to grasp the bend, shape the wire over the top jaw (photo 5), and swing it underneath to form a partial loop (photo 6).

3. Use chain-nose pliers or your fingers to wrap the wire in a tight coil down the stem (photo 7). Then trim the excess wire close to the wrap and use chain-nose pliers to tighten the wire end.

Note: You may notice that some project instructions say to bend the wire 45°, rather than 90°. This bend keeps the loop centered above the bead and prevents it from veering to one side just as well as the 90° bend does (photo 8).

Triangular Wraps

This wrap looks great on a bead that is drilled through the width or top drilled, or on a bicone you want to position horizontally.

1. Cut a piece of wire 2 inches (5.1 cm) long. With flat-nose pliers, bend the last ½ inch (1.3 cm) of the wire upward. Thread a bead onto the wire.

2. Fold up the other side of the wire until the pieces cross directly above the bead, creating a hat (figure 5).

3. Take the chain-nose pliers to the base of the longer wire, and bend it back down a bit. Use the round-nose pliers to make a simple loop (figure 6).

4. Finish the piece by wrapping the end of the longer wire around the base several times. Snip off the excess wire and file the end, or else tuck it underneath the last loop.

When attaching these beads, make sure the direction of the loop brings attention to the bead instead of the wire. If you've already completed your loop and it is not facing the direction you prefer, simply grip the loop with round-nose pliers and give it a small additional twist to make the loop either forward facing or side facing, whichever is needed for your piece. Following up with this small but important detail will allow the bead to be the focus of your design.

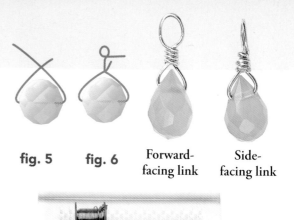

fig. 5   fig. 6   Forward-facing link   Side-facing link

Using Jigs

Jigs are especially handy because they allow you to quickly create multiple wire designs, all of them identical. A jig is basically a flat surface with equidistant holes. Place pegs in these holes to form the desired pattern, then wrap wire around them to form a looped wire design (photo 9). Be sure to experiment with cheap wire until you're pleased with the results of your jig work, then switch to precious-metal wire to make your jewelry design.

Finishing Off Wires

When you're done with a piece of wire, clip the tails, and press them down so no sharp ends stick out of your finished piece; these might scratch or stab you or snag your clothes. Then run your fingers across the area to check for sharp ends. If you find some, keep pressing them down and/or clip them a bit more. If necessary, file the tip of the wire with an emery board or a hand file.

photo 9

Opening and Closing Jump Rings

Always open a jump ring with two pairs of pliers, one positioned on each side of the split. Push one pair of pliers away from you, and pull the other one toward you (photo 10). This way the ring will be opened laterally, instead of horizontally, which can weaken the wire. You'll want to open any other wire loop you work the same way.

photo 10

Crimping

Crimping is one method for attaching wire to a finding.

1. String one crimp bead and then the finding. Pass the wire end back through the crimp bead in the opposite direction.

2. Next, slide the crimp bead against the finding so it's snug, but not so tight that the wire can't move freely. Squeeze the crimp bead in the U-shaped notch—the notch furthest from the tip—of the crimping pliers (photo 11).

photo 11

3. Rotate the crimp bead and nestle it into the front notch. Gently squeeze the bead so it collapses on itself into a nicely shaped tube (photo 12).

photo 12

Working with Chain

Chain is one of the simplest materials to use in jewelry making. The toughest part is deciding which type to use! After that, all you need to do is cut the chain and create your piece.

The lengths of chain you'll need for the projects are specified in each set of directions. Rulers are helpful, but you shouldn't always rely on them for determining the length of chain to cut. Instead, when working with multiple pieces of chain that are supposed to be the same length, count links. Use a ruler to measure just the first length of chain, then count the links in that segment, and count all additional chain segments to make absolutely certain that each one has exactly the same number of links. After you determine the right length for the piece you're making, pull out your trusty wire cutters and snip away.

To attach a chain to wire or a finding, slide one link of the chain (often an end link) onto a wire loop or finding. Generally, the chain is secured with wrapped wire.

Reaming Beads

If the hole in a bead is too small to fit onto a wire, head pin, or finding, you can make it larger. Semiprecious stones or artisan beads are ideal candidates for this process, but it's really not worth the effort to ream a seed bead, or any other inexpensive bead.

You can use a manual or electric bead reamer.

1. Stick the bead to a small piece of poster putty.

2. Gently push the reamer back and forth inside the hole, working only on half of the bead. Work slowly for maximum control, and do not push too hard. Keep the tip of the reamer wet. Tips are diamond-coated, and using the reamer dry will wear off the coating. If you're using a manual tool, you can work with the reamer submerged in a shallow bowl of water or held under running water. (*Never* do this with an electric reamer. Instead, dip the drill bit in a small cup of water whenever it feels like the bead is sticking.)

3. Remove the putty, flip the bead over, and stick the putty on the opposite side. Finish reaming the hole for the newly exposed opening.

Do *not* ream crystals. They shatter easily. Instead, choose a jump ring or wire to fit the hole. The jump ring size that fits in the crystal's hole will be sufficient to support the crystal and will be strong enough to last with regular, everyday wear.

Drilling Holes in Metal

Whether you're making a hole to string an item or making a rivet, the process is basically the same. You can use a flex shaft or an electric, handheld rotary tool. Although drilling a hole may take a few moments longer with a manual drill, you have more control with this tool.

1. Mark the hole position with a fine-tip permanent pen. (Some jewelers skip this step.) Do not mark the hole position too close to an edge, particularly when working with soft metal such as sterling silver, which can tear when drilled.

2. Place the charm or piece of metal on an anvil. Create a divot at the marked spot. You can do this by positioning the tip of an awl or a center punch at the hole mark and then tapping the top with a hammer.

3. You may want to clamp the item to a piece of wood to prevent the metal piece from spinning while drilling. Position the tip of the drill bit in the divot and begin drilling. Do not force the drill bit through the metal. Drill slowly and steadily, letting the drill do the work. For a thicker item, you might want to start with a drill bit that makes a hole smaller than you need. After creating the first hole, you can enlarge it with a drill bit of the desired finished size.

4. After drilling, smooth rough edges with a file, and then sand with sandpaper.

Polishing

Polish your jewelry with either a jewelry buffing cloth—sometimes called a rouge cloth—or papers, which are available from most jewelry suppliers. Before using any cleaning solution, test it on a scrap piece of wire first. A tumbler is an option for some pieces, but make sure you're familiar with its operation and know that many beads aren't suitable for the process.

photo 13

photo 14

Liver of Sulfur Patina

You can blacken silver, brass, or copper by dropping it into a solution of liver of sulfur. This simple procedure adds color and depth to your jewelry because the liver of sulfur darkens any surface design you've created and makes it more visible. Liver of sulfur has a strong odor, so you'll want to use it in a well-ventilated area or outside. Wear rubber gloves when you work with the solution.

1. In a glass bowl, dissolve a chunk of liver of sulfur in hot water.

2. Drop the piece of jewelry into the solution (photo 13). Leave the metal in the solution until it turns black, approximately one to two minutes. (If you leave the piece in the solution for too long, the black color becomes a thick crust that can flake off later.)

3. Use copper tongs to remove the piece from the solution (photo 14), and wash it in hot water, which helps the patina adhere.

You may need to repeat this process for a blacker tone. You can then leave the piece black, or rub it with an abrasive—steel wool, a coarse cleanser, or a green kitchen scrubby—to let the natural color of the metal come through the patina.

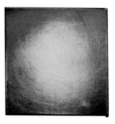

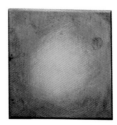

A liver-of-sulfur finish rubbed off (from top to bottom) sterling silver, copper, and brass

temple gate

Though this bracelet contains Chinese porcelain and Czech glass, its exotic design and Thai silver beads mark it as something you might encounter in a Bangkok market stall.

Designer: Andrea L. Stern

Finished Size: 7 inches (17.8 cm) in circumference; adjustable

Materials

10 head pins, each 3 inches (7.6 cm) long

32 Thai silver barrel beads, 4 x 3 mm

20 round Chinese porcelain beads, 6 mm

20 Thai silver puffy rondelle beads, 6 x 4 mm

10 coral glass barrel beads, 10 x 8 mm

15-inch (38.1 cm) length of bracelet wire

56 Czech glass round beads, 4 mm

22 teardrop silver puffy charms, 12 x 9 mm

Tools

Round-nose pliers

Ruler or tape measure

Wire cutters

Heavy-duty wire cutters for bracelet wire (optional)

Crimping pliers

Instructions

1. To make the connecting bars, take a head pin, and string one small silver barrel, a porcelain bead, one Thai silver rondelle, a coral barrel, a Thai silver rondelle, a porcelain bead, and a small silver barrel.

2. Use the round-nose pliers to make a simple loop at one end of the head pin by bending the wire 90°, approximately ¼ inch (6 mm) from the end, and then turning the loop. Slide the beads down to the loop, and make another simple loop at the other end of the pin.

3. Repeat steps 1 and 2 nine more times for a total of 10 bars.

4. Use wire cutters to cut the loop of the bracelet wire in half. Each piece is approximately 7½ inches (19 cm) in length.

Make a tiny loop at one end of the bracelet wire, and string as follows:
- *Round glass bead
- Small silver barrel

Repeat from * two more times, then continue as follows:
- *Round glass bead
- Puffy charm
- Round glass bead
- Connecting head pin bar

Repeat from * nine more times, then continue as follows:
- Round glass bead
- Puffy charm
- *Round glass bead
- Small silver barrel

Repeat from * two more times, and then end with a round glass bead.

5. Make a tiny loop and close the wire tightly. Crimping pliers are good for this.

On the second piece of wire, make a loop and string as follows:
- *Round glass bead
- Small silver barrel

Repeat from * two more times, then continue as follows:
- Round glass bead
- Puffy charm
- Round glass bead

6. Slide the wire through the bottom loop of your first connecting bar, and then string another round glass bead, a puffy charm, and another round glass bead.

7. Repeat step 8, sliding the wire through each connecting bar as you go. The wire will want to twist and fight you, but with a little perseverance and some maneuvering, the bracelet will come together.

8. Once all of your connecting bars are strung, string a glass bead, then your last puffy charm, and then follow the same bead/barrel pattern you used at the beginning of the wire in step 5. Make another tiny loop with the round-nose pliers, and close the loop with the crimping pliers.

ocean
waves

Use a jig to make the wire waves, then link them with abalone
and lapis lazuli for this bracelet inspired by the sea.

Designer: Valérie MacCarthy

Finished size: 7½ inches (19 cm) long

Materials

4 rectangular abalone beads, 15 mm

8 lapis lazuli beads, 6 mm

35-inch (88.9 cm) length of 22-gauge sterling silver wire

33-inch (83.8 cm) length of 24-gauge sterling silver wire

Sterling silver figure-eight lobster clasp

Tools

Jig

Round-nose pliers

Chain-nose pliers

Large rubberized round-nose pliers

Wire cutters

Instructions

1. Use the jig and the 22-gauge wire to make eight wire "waves." Use a three-loop peg spacing as shown in figure 1.

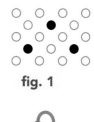

fig. 1

2. To create the waves, wrap the wire around the pegs following the directional pattern shown in figure 2.

fig. 2

3. After creating the wave shape, remove it from the jig. Using the chain-nose pliers, hold one of the side loops. Wrap one end of the wire around to secure the loop in place. Cut off the excess wire. Do the same for the loop on the other side (figure 3). You may need to pull the two ends slightly to make sure the center loop holds its shape. Then use the rubberized round-nose pliers to squeeze and flatten the wave as much as possible. Repeat this for all eight of the waves.

fig. 3

4. Using the round-nose pliers, make a loop in the 24-gauge wire about ¾ inch (1.9 cm) from the end. Slide the clasp onto this loop. Hold the loop with the chain-nose pliers, and then twist the wires around to secure. Cut off the shorter wire end. Slide on a 15-mm rectangular abalone bead and bend the wire 45°. Hold this wire with the round-nose pliers and wrap it around to make a loop.

5. Slide the center loop of a wave onto this wire loop, hold the loop with the chain-nose pliers, and wrap the wire around to secure. Cut off the excess wire.

6. Using the round-nose pliers, make a new loop in the 24-gauge wire about ¾ inch (1.9 cm) from the end. Slide the loop onto one of the side loops of the wave. Grab this loop with the chain-nose pliers and twist the wires together to secure. Cut off the shorter wire end.

7. Place a 6-mm lapis lazuli bead onto the wire, bend the wire 45°, and loop it around again. Slide this loop onto the side loop of another wire wave and wrap it closed using the chain-nose pliers. Cut off the excess wire.

8. Repeat steps 6 and 7 on the other side loop of the wave, ending up with two 6-mm lapis lazuli beads across from each other on the bracelet.

9. Repeat steps 4 through 8 three times to add the remaining wire waves and stones, sliding the wire through the center loop of the wave instead of through the clasp in step 4. Make sure the final wave is attached with its center loop facing out, as this loop will serve as a catch for the clasp. (Don't add another clasp here as described in step 4, because the wire loop will do just fine as a catch.)

river dance

Since every river-polished stone has its own shape and personality,
tailor the way you wrap each one to enhance its individuality.

Designer: Rachel M. Dow

Finished size: 7½ inches (19 cm) long

Materials

5 tumbled river stones, 14 to 16 mm in diameter

12-foot (3.7 m) length of 18-gauge dead-soft sterling silver wire

8-inch (20.3 cm) length of sterling silver chain-link bracelet with toggle

At least 11 sterling silver jump rings, 4 mm in diameter

Tools

Round-nose pliers

Chain-nose pliers

Instructions

1. Lay out the stones in the order you wish to place them on the bracelet, keeping in mind how their colors and shapes relate to each other.

2. Cut five pieces of wire, each 6¼ inches (15.9 cm) long. Leaving a tail 1 inch (2.5 cm) long at the top of the center stone, wrap the long end of the wire around it. Hold both the stone and wire firmly as you crisscross the wire. Once you've finished, wrap the working wire twice around the tail, then form a wrapped loop. Wrap the rest of the stones.

3. Determine where to hang the wrapped stones on the chain; they shouldn't be too close to the toggle ends. Attach the center stone first, hanging it from a short chain made from three linked jump rings. Stagger the lengths of the other stones by changing the number of jump rings from which they hang.

crystal
radiance

Whether you're new to wire wrapping or you're a pro at it, try out this simple yet charming bracelet featuring quartz beads and silver charms.

Designer: Wendy Remmers

Finished size: 8½ inches (21.6 cm) long

Materials

4 silver Bali beads, 15 mm

3 crystal quartz beads, 15 x 20 mm

14 daisy spacers, 5 mm

6 spacer beads, 4 mm (optional)

2-foot (61 cm) length of 22-gauge sterling silver wire

6 closed jump rings, 5 mm

Sterling silver toggle clasp, 20 mm

Tools

Flush cutters

Chain-nose pliers

Round-nose pliers

Designer's Tips

Buy a spool of inexpensive craft wire and practice your loop and wire wrapping skills until your loops are round and your wraps are consistent and tight. This will help increase your speed when wire wrapping a bracelet or necklace and save you money when you're using more expensive wire for the real thing.

Instructions

1. You'll build the bracelet from one end to the other. Cut a 3-inch (7.6 cm) piece of 22-gauge wire. Form a loop in one end, catch one half of the clasp in it, and then wire wrap the loop closed. Trim off any excess wire. String a daisy spacer, a Bali bead, and another daisy spacer onto the wire. Form a loop, catch a jump ring in it, and then wire wrap the loop closed. Trim off the excess wire. This is the first wrapped loop link.

2. Cut a 3-inch (7.6 cm) piece of 22-gauge wire. Form a loop, catch it in the jump ring of the previously made wrapped loop link, and then wrap the loop closed. String on a daisy spacer, a quartz bead, and a second daisy spacer. Form a loop, catch a jump ring in it, and then wire wrap the loop closed. Trim off the excess wire. You've now made the second wrapped loop link in a chain.

3. Add five more wrapped loop links to the chain, alternating Bali beads and quartz beads. Before you close the second wrapped loop of the seventh wrapped loop link, catch the other half of the clasp in it.

sunset

Shell pearls in vivid peaches
and pinks combine to create an
artistic display in this eye-catching,
multi-strand bracelet.

Materials

Designer: Valérie MacCarthy

Finished size: 7⅝ inches (19.4 cm) long

3 shell pearls in bright pink, 16 mm

4 shell pearls in peach, 14 mm

4 shell pearls in medium pink, 12 mm

18 shell pearls in light pink, 8 mm

20 shell pearls in lightest pink, 4 mm

24 smoky quartz beads, 4 mm

20 gold-filled beads, 2 mm

4 gold-filled beads, 3 mm

Gold-filled four-strand slide clasp

6-inch (15.2 cm) length of gold-filled chain, 1.5 mm

38-inch (96.5 cm) length of 24-gauge gold-filled wire

Tools

Chain-nose pliers

Round-nose pliers

Wire cutters

Ruler

Instructions

1. To make this bracelet, start from the outside and work your way in. Separate the two slide clasp pieces while making the bracelet, always being careful to attach each strand to the correct loop. Using the round-nose pliers and the 24-gauge wire, create a loop about ¾ inch (1.9 cm) from the end of the wire. Slide the loop through one of the outer loops on one of the pieces of the slide clasp. Hold the wire loop with the chain-nose pliers and twist the wire around. Cut off the shorter wire end.

2. Slide on the following beads: one 4-mm smoky quartz bead, one 2-mm gold-filled bead, one 4-mm shell pearl bead, one 2-mm gold-filled bead, and one 12-mm shell pearl bead.

3. Bend the wire about 45° and, using the round-nose pliers, make a loop in the wire. Slide the chain onto the loop. Hold the loop with the chain-nose pliers and wrap the wire around to secure. Cut off the excess wire.

4. Cut off all the chain, leaving only one link attached. (If you prefer, you can use a jump ring here instead of one link of the chain.) Using your fingers, curve this just-finished beaded wire to form a slight outward-facing curve (figure 1).

fig. 1

5. Using the round-nose pliers, make a new loop in the wire approximately ¾ inch (1.9 cm) from the end. Slide the wire through the one link of chain you attached in step 4. Hold the loop with the chain-nose pliers and wrap the wire around. Cut off the shorter wire end.

6. Slide on the following beads: one 4-mm smoky quartz bead, one 2-mm gold-filled bead, one 4-mm shell pearl bead, one 3-mm gold-filled bead, one 4-mm shell pearl bead, one 2-mm gold-filled bead, and one 4-mm smoky quartz bead.

7. Repeat steps 3 and 4 of looping the wire, attaching it to one chain link (or use a jump ring, if you prefer), and curving the beaded wire (figure 2).

fig. 2

8. Make a loop in the wire using the round-nose pliers. Slide it through the one link of chain. Holding the loop with the chain-nose pliers, wrap the wire around to secure it. Cut off the shorter wire end.

9. Slide one 4-mm smoky quartz bead, one 14-mm shell pearl bead, and one smoky quartz bead onto the wire.

10. Repeat steps 3 and 4 of looping the wire, attaching it to the chain or a jump ring, and curving the beaded wire.

11. Loop the wire again using the round-nose pliers, slide it through the link of chain, and wrap the wire around with the chain-nose pliers. Cut off the shorter wire end.

12. Slide on the following beads: one 4-mm shell pearl bead, one 2-mm gold-filled bead, one 4-mm smoky quartz bead, one 8-mm shell pearl bead, one 4-mm smoky quartz bead, one 2-mm gold-filled bead, and one 4-mm shell pearl bead.

13. Repeat steps 3 and 4 of looping the wire, attaching it to the chain or a jump ring, and curving the beaded wire.

14. You've now arrived just past the midpoint of the first strand. Make three more curved beaded sections before attaching this strand to the opposite end of the slide clasp. For these beaded sections, repeat the bead sequence used in steps 9, 6, and 2, in that order, but attach the section from step 2 in reverse order, so it mirrors the other end of the strand.

15. After making the final curve, attach the strand to the slide clasp; make sure the pieces of the clasp are oriented as shown when you attach the strand (figure 3).

fig. 3

16. You've now finished the first strand. Repeat this entire strand, working steps 1 through 15, for the other outer loops of the slide clasp (figure 4). Be especially careful to attach each strand to the correct loop of the clasp.

fig. 4

17. Now make the inner strands of the bracelet. Make a loop with 24-gauge wire using the round-nose pliers. Slide this loop through one of the inner loops on one of the pieces of the slide clasp.

18. Hold the wire loop with the chain-nose pliers and twist the wire around. Cut off the shorter wire end.

19. Make a new loop in the wire using round-nose pliers. Holding this second loop with the chain-nose pliers, wrap the wire around the twist you made in step 18. Cut off the excess wire.

20. Make a new loop in the wire ¾ inch (1.9 cm) from the end. Slide this loop through the twisted wire loop attached to the slide clasp. Using the chain-nose pliers, hold this loop and twist the wires around. Cut off the shorter wire end.

21. Slide on one 8-mm shell pearl bead (figure 5) and make a new loop in the wire. Place ⅜ inch (1 cm) of chain on the loop, hold that loop with the chain-nose pliers, and wrap the wire around to secure the chain.

fig. 5

22. Repeat steps 17 through 21 for the other inner loop on the slide clasp.

23. Create a new loop with the wire and place both chain ends on this loop. Hold the loop with the chain-nose pliers and wrap the wire around to secure. Cut off the shorter wire end.

24. Slide one 16-mm shell pearl bead onto the wire. Loop the wire again, attaching two more ⅜-inch (9.5 mm) chain lengths to this loop before you secure it.

25. Make a new loop with the wire and attach it to one of the pieces of chain you added in step 24. Twist the wire around to secure the loop and cut off the shorter wire end. Slide on one 8-mm shell pearl bead and loop the wire again. Attach another ⅜-inch (1 cm) length of chain. Wrap the wire around to secure the loop and cut off the excess wire. Repeat this step with the other piece of chain.

26. Repeat steps 24 and 25 two more times to arrive at the other end of the bracelet.

27. Make twisted wire loop links to attach each strand to the slide clasp (figure 6).

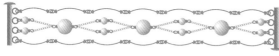

fig. 6

28. Next, attach the central strand of the bracelet to the outer strands. Make a loop with the 24-gauge wire. Slide this loop through one of the loops at either side of the 16-mm shell pearl bead in the center. Using the chain-nose pliers, hold the loop and wrap the wires around. Cut off the shorter wire end.

29. Slide one 8-mm shell pearl bead onto the wire and loop the wire again. Make this loop perpendicular to the first loop, instead of both facing the same way. (When completed, the loop should appear as in figure 7.)

fig. 7

30. Slide this loop through the two loops from the outer strands that are joined by the single link of chain. The little chain link that was there to hold it all together will now be encircled by this new wire loop. Wrap the wire to secure the loop and cut off the excess wire (figure 8).

fig. 8

31. Repeat steps 28 through 30 three more times until all sides of the center bead are attached.

32. Using one 4-mm shell pearl bead and one 8-mm shell pearl bead, make the same connections as in steps 28 through 30, placing these sections on the inner side of the two remaining 16-mm beads (figure 9).

fig. 9

nexus

Dozens of intertwined jump rings form chain mail links,
which enclose red carnelian beads for a clustered feel.

Designer: Rachel Sims

Finished size: 21 inches (53 cm) long

Materials

64 aluminum 18-gauge jump rings,
7/16 inch (1.1 cm)

6 aluminum 18-gauge jump rings,
1/8 inch (3 mm)

Silver toggle clasp, 8 mm

16 carnelian beads, 6 mm

Tools

2 pairs chain-nose or flat-nose pliers

Instructions

1. Open half of the large jump rings. Completely close the other half of the large jump rings.

2. Open five of the small jump rings. Completely close one of the small jump rings.

3. Place a small closed jump ring and the loop portion of the toggle clasp on a small open jump ring, and then close that jump ring.

4. Place two large closed jump rings on an open large jump ring. Weave the open jump ring through the small jump ring that is not attached to the toggle.

5. Double the single large open ring. That is, thread another open large jump ring through the two large closed rings and also through the small jump ring, and then close it. At this point, you should have the loop end of the toggle followed by two small jump rings followed by two doubled sets of large jump rings.

6. Hold the piece near the small jump rings so the small jump rings and the toggle are hanging at the bottom. Gently fold back the top large jump rings, and insert a bead between the two large jump rings at the bottom.

7. Bring the top-most large jump rings (bracketing the bead) back to meet at the center, and thread an open large jump ring through both of them. Note: Make sure that when you add a bead to each cage, the jump rings do not get caught under the bead. They should bracket the bead on each side, hemming it in securely.

8. Add two closed jump rings to the open large jump ring, and then close the large jump ring. Double the open large jump ring through the two closed rings.

9. Repeat steps 6 through 8 until you've used all jump rings and beads or until the desired bracelet length is met.

10. To finish the bracelet, thread a small open ring through the last set of large jump rings. Add a small closed jump ring, and then close the open small jump ring.

11. Weave another open small ring through the last attached small jump ring, and add the bar end of the toggle clasp. Close the small jump ring.

loop de loop

The muted, cool tones of these delicate glass rings are offset with brass tones for a classic French look.

Designer: Kaari Meng

Finished size: 6½ inches (16.6 cm) long

Materials

8 brass jump rings, 5 mm

12 brass jump rings, 8 mm

2 Peking glass oval rings, 18 x 25 mm

3 Peking glass round rings, 20 mm

Brass spring ring clasp, 24 mm

Tools

2 pairs of flat-nose pliers

Finished size: 6½ inches (16.6 cm) long

Materials

25 brass jump rings, 3 mm

9 green and blue glass round rings, 14 mm

Brass spring ring clasp, 12 mm

Tools

2 pairs of flat-nose pliers

Instructions for the version with large glass rings

1. Link the spring ring clasp to three 5-mm jump rings. Link the jump rings to the 8-mm jump rings, and then link onto the round glass ring. Attach the opposite side of the round glass ring to a second 8-mm jump ring.

2. Connect the next 8-mm jump ring using a 5-mm jump ring. Note: The 8-mm jump ring will then connect to the oval glass ring. Continue connecting the rings together using a 5-mm jump ring between each 8-mm jump ring.

3. Once you have linked five glass rings together, attach the remaining three 8-mm jump rings to the remaining round glass ring.

Instructions for the version with small glass rings

1. Link the spring clasp to a 3-mm jump ring and attach to a 14-mm glass ring. Connect three more 3-mm jump rings to the glass ring. Before closing the third jump ring, connect to another glass ring.

2. Continue connecting the rings together using three 3-mm jump rings. There's no need to add a large jump ring at the end—the clasp can connect to one of the glass rings to close the bracelet.

countless

Create this easily adaptable bracelet using purple and green gemstones, or select other color and stone combinations to match your mood.

Designer: Valérie MacCarthy

Finished size: 7¼ inches (18.4 cm) long

Materials

18 amethyst round beads, 8 mm

12 peridot round beads, 6 mm

13 peridot oval beads, 8 mm

16 gold-filled beads, 3 mm

Gold-filled four-strand slide clasp

55-inch (1.4 m) length of gold-filled chain, 3.5 mm

88-inch (2.2 m) length of 24-gauge gold-filled wire

Tools

Chain-nose pliers

Round-nose pliers

Wire cutters

Ruler

Instructions

1. Separate the two slide clasp pieces while making the bracelet, always being careful to attach each strand to the correct loop. Begin by making wire loop links to attach the chain to the slide clasp. Loop the 24-gauge wire around the round-nose pliers about ¾ inch (1.9 cm) from the end of the wire. To make the loop larger, wrap the wire around the pliers at a thicker part of the jaws. After you've made the first loop, thread the slide clasp onto it. Also place the chain on this loop before wrapping the wire around to secure it. Hold this loop with the chain-nose pliers and twist the wire around to secure. Cut off the shorter wire end. *Note:* When placing the chain on the other three wire loops that will be connected to the slide clasp, always be sure to place the chain on the same side of the loop to maintain consistency (figure 1).

This chain is always on the same side.

fig. 1

2. Hold the remaining wire with the round-nose pliers and loop it again. Cut the attached chain to about ½ inch (1.3 cm) in length so that you can attach a new piece. Slip a new chain length onto the other wire loop. Hold the loop with the chain-nose pliers and wrap the wire around the twist you made in step 1. Cut off the excess wire.

3. Now for the fun part! This bracelet requires you to experiment. The stones are randomly placed throughout, which means the length of the chain between each stone is completely up to you. For the bracelet shown, I varied the length of chain between the stones from a single link to about 1 inch (2.5 cm).

4. Attach a stone or stones (I don't recommend more than two) to the end of the first chain by making a loop in the wire about ¾ inch (1.9 cm) from the end. Attach this loop to the end of the chain. Hold this loop with the chain-nose pliers and twist the wires around to secure. Place a stone or stones onto the wire, bend the wire 45°, and loop it again using the round-nose pliers. Attach a new length of chain onto this loop and hold the loop with the chain-nose pliers. Wrap the wire around to secure and cut off the excess wire.

5. Repeat steps 3 and 4 on both chains until you reach the length you need and are ready to attach it to the other half of the slide clasp. *Note:* The top chain on the first end should remain the top chain on this end, too. Therefore, the top chain will need to be slightly longer because it needs to reach the first loop of the wire link (figure 2).

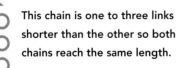

This chain is one to three links shorter than the other so both chains reach the same length.

fig. 2

6. Repeat step 1 but in reverse, attaching the bottom (shorter) end to the looped wire first. Twist it to secure. Using the round-nose pliers, bend the wire a second time and slide it through the slide clasp. Place the second chain on this same loop. Hold the loop with the chain-nose pliers. Wrap the wire around the twist you just made and cut off the excess wire. You've finished the first length of the bracelet.

7. Repeat steps 1 through 6 three more times to complete the bracelet. As you work, study your completed sections to make sure you're not placing similar stones too close together. Plan the length of the chain segments so the stones are interspersed throughout.

wire & crystal

Add sparkle to your wrist with this exotic cuff made
of wrapped coils and beads around a wire frame.

Designer: Wendy Witchner

Finished size: 7¾ inches (19.7 cm) long

● Materials

62 assorted color crystal bicone beads, 4 to 6 mm

38 sterling silver Bali-style spacer beads and bead caps in various shapes, 3 to 7 mm

12-inch (30.5 cm) length of 20-gauge round sterling silver wire

36-inch (91.4 cm) length of 22-gauge twisted sterling silver wire

36-inch (91.4 cm) length of 24-gauge half-hard round sterling silver wire (for wrapping)

16-inch (40.6 cm) length of 14-gauge dead-soft round sterling silver wire (for cuff frame)

Liver of sulfur

● Tools

Wire cutters

Chain-nose pliers

Round-nose pliers

Planishing hammer

Texturizing hammer

Steel block

Wire brush or tumbler

Bracelet mandrel or frozen juice can

Metal hand file

● Instructions

Making the Coils

1. Tightly coil the twisted wire down the length of the 20-gauge wire. Trim the tails close to the coil.

2. Dip the coiled wire into a liver of sulfur solution, rinse, and brush.

3. Slide the coil off the end of the 20-gauge wire and trim off a 6-mm length. Repeat to make 38 coiled tubes in a variety of lengths, each between 4 and 10 mm long (figure 1). Set the coils aside.

fig. 1

Making the Frame

1. Use your fingers to bend the 14-gauge wire in half, making a soft V shape. The wire sides should be about ¼ inch (6 mm) apart. Use chain-nose pliers to make a 45° bend in each wire about ⅜ inch (1 cm) inch up from the point so the wire ends are farther apart. Make a simple loop at each end of the wire (figure 2).

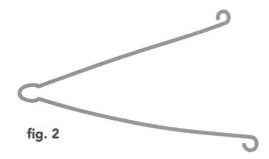

fig. 2

2. Use the hammers and steel block to slightly flatten and texturize the 14-gauge wire.

3. Dip the wire into a liver of sulfur solution, rinse, and brush.

Wrapping the Frame

1. Coil one end of the 24-gauge wire several times to the 14-gauge wire at a spot on the frame just near one of the simple loops.

2. String one 6-mm crystal bead and one 7-mm coil. Draw the beaded wire across toward the other simple loop, gently pull both simple loops together, and make two or three wraps around the 18-gauge wire from back to front.

3. String one 6-mm crystal bead, one 4-mm bead cap, and one 8-mm coil. Draw the beaded wire across to the other side of the 14-gauge wire and make two or three wraps from back to front (figure 3).

4. Gently wrap the 14-gauge wire form over the bracelet mandrel or juice can to form a cuff shape.

5. Repeat step 3, stringing beads and coils and wrapping the wire around the opposite side of the cuff. As you move toward the center of the cuff, increase the number of beads and coils used so that by the time you reach the center, the cuff is about 1½ inches (3.8 cm) wide. Decrease beads as you move toward the other end of the cuff.

6. Once you reach the 45° bend you made when forming the cuff, finish the wire by coiling it several times around one side of the 14-gauge wire.

7. Trim the tail wires at each end of the cuff. Use chain-nose pliers to squeeze the beginning and ending coils tight so no wire can abrade the skin. File the wire ends as necessary.

fig. 3

copper jangle

Wire-looped charms hang from a chain, bone beads hang from the ends of the charms, and the whole design hangs together beautifully.

Designer: Cindy Kinerson

Finished size: 7¾ inches (19.7 cm) long

Materials

5-foot (1.5 m) length of 20-gauge copper wire

7-inch (17.8 cm) length of copper link chain

21 assorted bone beads

6 red horn spacer beads

5 gold horn spacer beads

6 copper beads

4 red-colored white heart beads

Copper toggle clasp

Tools

Wire cutters

Ruler or tape measure

Round-nose pliers

2 pairs of chain-nose pliers

Instructions

1. Use the wire cutters to cut the copper wire in 3-inch (7.6 cm) lengths. You'll need as many pieces of wire as you have links in your chain.

2. To make the charms: Thread the first inch (2.5 cm) of one 3-inch (7.6 cm) length of wire through a bone bead. Bend the 1-inch section of the wire at a 90° angle, and wrap it twice around the other approximately 2-inch (5.1 cm) section of the wire. Place one of the

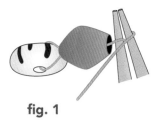

fig. 1

spacer, copper, or white heart beads above the wrapped wire, and then use your round-nose pliers to form a loop with the straight end of the wire (figure 1). Make two wraps below the loop, and trim off the excess with the wire cutters. Use your chain-nose pliers to help adjust the wire wraps so they're tight. Repeat with all of the bone beads.

3. To assemble the bracelet: Open the first link of the copper chain with your chain-nose pliers, and slide on half of the toggle clasp and one charm. Close the link. Add a charm for each link of the chain. When you reach the last link, slide on one charm and the other half of the toggle clasp. Close the link.

Designer's Tip

If you can't find copper chain with links that open, use regular chain and string the copper wire through each chain link before making the second loop.

simple strands

These bead and wire bracelets are simple to make and fun to mix and match.
Make extra wire links and use them in matching earrings and necklaces.

Designer: Gary Helwig

Finished size: 7⅞ inches (20 cm) long

Materials

4-inch (10.2 cm) length of 18-gauge wire*

30-inch (76.2 cm) length of 22-gauge wire

4-inch (10.2 cm) length of 24-gauge wire (optional)

8 beads (crystals or pearls), 6 mm

Clasp

6-inch (15.2 cm) length of medium or fine chain

* Any wire will do, but half-hard wire works best because it will require less hardening when the wire component is complete.

Tools

Round-nose pliers

Bent chain-nose pliers

Flush cutter

Small jig with two small pegs and two large pegs, ³⁄₁₆ inches (5 mm) recommended

Chasing hammer and anvil (optional)

Nylon jaw pliers (optional)

Instructions

1. Straighten the 18-gauge wire. Using round-nose pliers, make a loop large enough to fit over the small metal pegs on the jig on one end of the wire.

2. Position two metal pegs and two large pegs in the jig (see photo 1).

3. Place the initial loop in the 18-gauge wire on one of the small metal pegs in the jig and wrap the wire as shown. Push the wire down while wrapping, holding the wire straight.

4. Remove the wire from the jig and cut the excess wire tail with flush cutters (see photo 2).

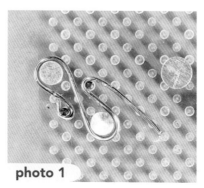

photo 1

photo 2

5. Close the final loop with bent chain-nose pliers. At this point the piece can be used as is, or, optionally (and recommended), it can be hardened by hammering it on an anvil with a chasing hammer (see photo 3). A final option is to wrap 24-gauge wire around the middle of the piece to further strengthen it. The unit you've just finished is called a Flemish Spiral and is the centerpiece of the bracelet. The bracelet is built out from the center.

6. Cut six pieces of chain approximately ⅜ inches (1 cm) each.

7. Using the 22-gauge wire and a 6-mm bead, make a wrapped bead link on one end of the Flemish Spiral. Connect the initial end of the wrapped bead link around one end of the Flemish Spiral and wrap that end closed. Add the 6-mm bead and begin making the other end of the wrapped bead link. Before wrapping the other end of the wrapped bead link closed, connect it to the end link on one piece

of chain. Once the chain has been added, complete the wrapped bead link by wrapping it closed.

8. Make two more wrapped bead links between the end of the chain and two more pieces of chain.

9. Make a fourth wrapped bead link between the end of the last piece of chain and half of the clasp.

10. Repeat steps 7 through 9 on the other end of the Flemish Spiral to make the other half of the bracelet.

Designer's Tip

Strengthening the Wire

For durability, it's important to take the time to temper, or harden, the wrapped wire. Metal gets harder as it's used—the molecules strengthen their bond to each other. By hammering the wire loops and coils after they are made with a smooth leather or nylon hammer, you'll strengthen the wire and help it hold its shape.

photo 3

circles & squares

Although most of its materials can be found at a hardware store rather than a high-end bead shop, this bracelet exudes fine style. This version features flat square pearls, but coins would work well, too.

Designer: Pat Evans

Finished size: 7¾ inches (19.7 cm) long

Materials

5 flat square rose-copper freshwater pearls, 12 mm

5 copper washers, outside diameter 1 inch (2.5 cm), inside diameter ⅝ inch (1.6 cm)

15-inch (38.1 cm) length of 22-gauge, dead-soft, round copper wire

33-inch (83.8 cm) length of 16-gauge, dead-soft, round copper wire

Tools

0000 steel wool

Tumbler with stainless steel shot and burnishing liquid (optional)

Flush cutters

Bent-tip chain-nose pliers

2 pairs of chain-nose pliers

Round-nose pliers

⅜-inch (1 cm) dowel, 4 inches (10.2 cm)

Chasing hammer

Bench block

Instructions

1. Clean the washers and remove the sharp edges on the underside by polishing them with steel wool or by tumbling them for 30 to 60 minutes. Dry the washers and set them aside.

2. Straighten and smooth the 22-gauge wire by pulling it through the steel wool. Cut the wire into five 3-inch (7.6 cm) pieces. Set them aside.

3. String one pearl onto a piece of 22-gauge wire. Slide the pearl to the middle of the wire and center a copper washer horizontally underneath the pearl.

4. Use your non-dominant hand to keep the pearl and washer in place as you grasp one wire end and make a sharp bend down the side and underneath the washer. Use bent-tip chain-nose pliers to guide the wire up through the center of the washer (figure 1). Make one tight wrap around the wire as in a wrapped loop (figure 2). Repeat this step for the other wire end. Finish seating the pearl by making a wrap with one wire end; repeat on the other side. This will help you easily center the pearl inside the washer (figure 3). Trim any excess wire and use chain-nose pliers to tighten the wraps. Repeat with the remaining 22-gauge wire, washers, and pearls to make five beaded links in all. Set them aside.

fig. 1

fig. 2

fig. 3

5. Cut a 3-inch (7.6 cm) length of 16-gauge wire and set it aside. Use the rest of the 16-gauge wire to make 19 jump rings in all. If you have extra jump rings, select only the roundest ones for this project.

6. Hammer each jump ring two or three times on its front and back. If the ring opens as you hammer, gently reshape it using the same technique as for opening and closing jump rings. Set the jump rings aside.

7. Straighten and polish the 3-inch (7.6 cm) length of 16-gauge wire cut in step 5. Use round-nose pliers to form a ¼-inch (6 mm) loop at one end. Shape the center of the wire over the dowel in a *U* shape. Form another, slightly smaller, loop on the straight end of the wire (figure 4). Hammer this wire fish-hook clasp to flatten and harden the metal.

fig. 4

8. Position the beaded links on the work surface so the 22-gauge wires line up. Use two jump rings to attach the large loop of the clasp to the left side of the first beaded link, one jump ring on each side of the wrapped loop.

9. Attach two jump rings to the right side of the previous beaded link. Open two more jump rings and use them to connect the two jump rings just added and the left side of the next beaded link in the line up. Repeat until you've attached all the links. Finish by adding one jump ring to the left side of the last link.

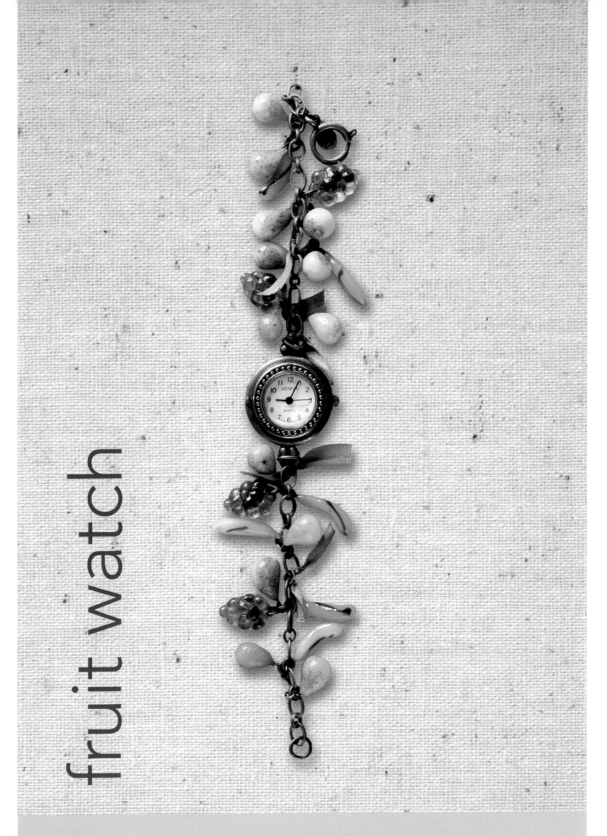

fruit watch

This is a fun twist on an old idea. The watch face is actually tied to the charm bracelet using bits of ribbon.

Designer: Kaari Meng

Finished size: 6¾ inches (17.5 cm) long

Materials

2 glass apples embedded with wire, 6 mm

6 glass bananas embedded with wire, 6 x 18 mm

4 glass grapes, 9 x 14 mm

10 glass pears embedded with wire, 9 x 14 mm

7-inch (17.8 cm) length of brass cable chains

6-inch (15.2 cm) length of silk ribbon, 5 mm

Brass jump ring, 8 mm

13 brass jump rings, 5 mm

Brass spring ring clasp, 12 mm

Watch face, 25 mm

Tools

Needle-nose pliers

Wire cutters

Instructions

1. Cut the chain in half. Cut and loop all the glass fruit with embedded wire. Attach a 5-mm jump ring the to side hole in each grape.

2. Attach a cluster of fruit—grape, apple, and pear—to a second 5-mm jump ring. Connect the fruit cluster to the second link on the chain. Continue assembling the fruit clusters—apple, banana, and pear—on the 5-mm jump rings. Connect to every other link on the chain.

3. Attach four clusters of fruit to each piece of chain. Cut the ribbon in half and thread through the link on the bottom of the watch face. Thread the same length of ribbon through the last link on the chain. Repeat on opposite side and tie both ribbon ends into a tight knot so that the watch face is connected to the chain with the clustered fruit.

4. Open the remaining 5-mm jump ring and connect the clasp to opposite end of the chain. Open the 8-mm jump ring and connect to opposite end of chain.

Designer's Tip

There are all sorts of wonderful gold watches in antique shops or maybe even in your own jewelry box. Consider removing an old watch face from its strap and using it for this project.

charming

Craft a truly elegant charm bracelet with iridescent coin pearls in soft shades of white, pink, and gray.

Designer: Valérie MacCarthy

Finished size: 7⅛ inches (18.1 cm) long

Materials

9 white coin pearls, 10 mm

6 soft pink coin pearls, 12 mm

3 gray coin pearls, 12 mm

18 sterling silver ball-end head pins, 1 inch (2.5 cm) long

Sterling silver lobster clasp

6½-inch (16.5 cm) length of sterling silver chain, 1.5 mm

2-inch (5.1 cm) length of 24-gauge sterling silver wire

Tools

Chain-nose pliers

Round-nose pliers

Wire cutters

Large rubberized round-nose pliers

Designer's Tip

For a project such as this one that is made with a long length of chain, I recommend not cutting the chain to the specified length until you've worked to the other end. All chains are slightly different, and you'll want to have the flexibility of cutting the chain to exactly the right length for the bracelet after you've attached all of the beads or stones.

Instructions

1. Using round-nose pliers, make a loop in the wire by holding it about ¾ inch (1.9 cm) from the end and wrapping the wire around. Slide the clasp onto this loop. Hold the loop with chain-nose pliers and twist the wires around to secure the clasp. Cut off the shorter wire end. Using round-nose pliers, bend the wire 45° and create a new loop. Slide one end of the chain onto it, holding it with the chain-nose pliers, and wrap the wire around to secure. Cut off the excess wire.

2. Select a 12-mm pearl and slide it onto a ball-end head pin. With the pearl in place, bend the head pin 45°. Hold it with round-nose pliers and loop it. Slide the head pin loop through the second link in the chain, adjacent to the one connected to the clasp. With the chain-nose pliers, hold the loop on the head pin and wrap it around to secure the loop. Cut off the excess wire. The first pearl is now in place (figure 1).

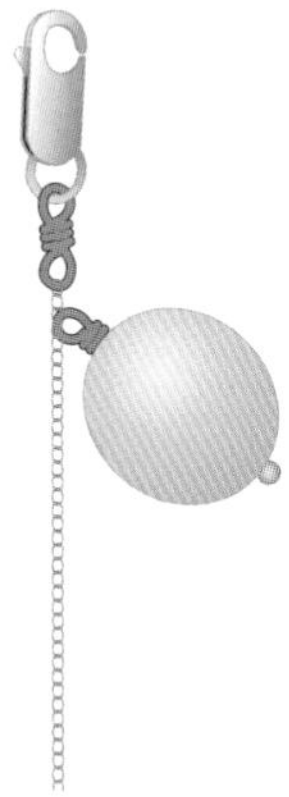

fig. 1

3. Slide a 10-mm pearl onto a head pin. Bend the head pin and loop it around as done in step 2. String it onto one of the links in the chain, six to eight links from the previous pearl. Wrap the head pin around and cut off the excess. *Note:* From this point on, always leave an odd number of links between each pearl. Make sure the pearls fall evenly from the chain by attaching each on the same side of the chain link.

4. Add the remaining pearls using the method in step 3. Alternate the placement of the 10-mm white pearls with the 12-mm pink and gray pearls as desired. Wrap the bracelet around your wrist to make sure the chain length is a good fit. Keep in mind that it will be slightly longer after you attach the catch for the clasp. Add extra pearls to create more length, if necessary. Cut the chain to your desired length.

5. Make a catch for the clasp by making a new loop in the wire. Slide this loop through the link following your last hanging pearl. Hold the loop with the chain-nose pliers and twist the wires around to secure. Cut off the shorter wire end.

6. Using the rubberized round-nose pliers, wrap the wire to form a large loop. Hold this loop firmly in the same tool and wrap the wire around the twist made in step 6 to secure. Cut off the excess wire.

dichroic brilliance

Designer: Geri Omohundro

Finished size: 7 inches (17.8 cm) long

Materials

15-inch (38.1 cm) length of 21-gauge gold-filled, half-hard square wire, or 21-gauge full-hard square silver wire

6½-inch (16.5 cm) length of 20-gauge gold-filled, dead-soft square wire, or 18-gauge dead-soft square silver wire

10-inch (25.4 cm) length of 21-gauge gold-filled, half-round wire, or 21-gauge half-round silver wire

Gold dichroic bead and two 4-mm topaz beads for upright bracelet, or rectangular fused glass disk or bead for flush bracelet

Tools

Pin vise or c-clamp

Round-nose pliers

Flat-nose pliers

Wire cutters

Tape

Polishing cloth

Emery board

Dichroic glass is made by applying a special coating treatment to the glass. The designer for this project made the beads as well. If you want to step up your wire-wrapping skills, try your hands at these twists and bundles.

Instructions

1. Place one end of the 15-inch (38.1 cm) length of wire in the vise and straighten by pulling the polishing cloth down the length of the wire several times. *Note:* The instructions for both bracelets are the same until step 7.

2. Place the 6½-inch (16.5 cm) length of wire in the vise ¼ inch (6 mm) and grasp it with the flat-nose pliers ¼ inch (6 mm) from the other end. Twist until you have a nice, even, fine pattern and leave the ends untwisted.

3. Bend the 15-inch (38.1 cm) length of wire in half using the round-nose pliers, making a loop about halfway up the pliers. Add the twisted wire to the middle of the 15-inch (38.1 cm) wire, holding ¼ inch (6 mm) in from the loop end. Wrap tape around the wire bundle about 2 inches (5.1 cm) and 5 inches (12.7 cm) from the loop to prevent the wires from twisting as you wrap them.

4. Using the 10-inch (25.4 cm) wire, make an angled bend at the end of the flat-nose pliers. Hook the bend over the bundle ½ inch (1.3 cm) from the loop (¼ inch (6 mm) from the twisted wire end). Grasp the hook and wire bundle with the flat-nose pliers and firmly wrap the half-round wire around the bundle five times, keeping the bundle straight and ending in the back. Snip the half-round wire and bevel-file with the emery board, and then press it against the wire.

5. Grasp the end of the twisted wire and bend back over the inside of your first wrap. As you work, bend the tip of the wire down, then press against the wrap to secure the end of the twisted wire.

6. Add two more wire wraps about 1 inch (2.5 cm) apart. You should have one wrap about ½ inch (1.3 cm) from the ends, one wrap close to each side of the bead area, and one wrap centered between the end and the bead wrap.

7. At this point you are about 3 inches (7.6 cm) into the project. Remove the tape on the 5-inch (12.7 cm) mark. Slightly bend out the outer wires and slide your beads along the center twisted wire. Check and center the beads, and then pull the wire bundle snug around them. You may wish to use round- or flat-nose pliers to help you make a symmetrical bend around the beads, depending on their shape. To make the fused glass bracelet, rout the glass (see Designer's Tip), then run the twisted center wire over, under, or through the bead hole depending on your preference.

8. Tape the wire bundle in two places again to hold the wires straight. Wire wrap next to the beads to hold them tight. Center the next wire wrap between the bead wrap and the end wrap. The end wrap should be ¼ inch (6 mm) in from the end of the twisted wire.

9. Bend the twisted wire back over the bundle as in step 5. About ½ inch (1.3 cm) of wire should remain at the end. Pinch these together with the flat-nose pliers and snip to even. File the edge square, then grasp with round-nose pliers and bend the wire into a J shape to form the clasp.

10. Shape the bracelet to form an oval by grasping the ends and slowly bending them toward each other as you brace the middle against a table. Use your fingers to keep tension on the whole piece so that it doesn't kink.

Designer's Tip

Routing Beads

Routing a groove holds the wire secure while allowing you to make almost invisible wire wraps. Working with a jewelry grinding bit and a compatible handheld power tool, set the bit so the groove will cut in the middle of the bead's edge. Grind into the edge of the bead just the thickness of your chosen wire. Clean off any dust.

dangling bangles

A simple wire technique is used to create this elegant
bracelet that changes with each movement of the wrist.

Designer: Mary Hettmansperger

Finished size: 8 inches (20.3 cm) long

Materials

39 to 42 light amber crystal cube beads, 4 mm

75 to 81 dark charcoal brown crystal bicone beads, 4 mm

39 to 42 black crystal round beads, 3 mm

7- to 8-foot (2.1 to 2.4 m) length of 20-gauge half-hard sterling silver wire

39 to 42 sterling silver head pins, 2 inches (5.1 cm)

Three-strand sterling silver slide-lock clasp

Tools

Wire cutters

Chain-nose pliers

Round-nose pliers

Designer's Tip

The bracelet shown fits an average wrist. Keep in mind that for a larger or smaller bracelet you may need to add or subtract links and bead dangles to get the proper fit.

Instructions

1. Cut 36 pieces of wire, each 2½ inches (6.4 cm) long. Set aside.

2. Use one head pin to string one cube bead, one bicone bead, and one round bead. Make a wrapped loop to secure the beads. Repeat to make 39 bead dangles. Set aside.

3. Begin a wrapped loop about one-third of the way down a piece of the cut wire. Before making the wrap, attach the loop to one of the bead dangles and to one of the holes on half of the clasp (figure 1). Complete the wrap.

fig. 1

4. String one bicone bead and make a wrapped loop on the other end of the wire to complete the link. The link should be about ¾ inch (1.9 cm) long.

5. As in step 3, begin a wrapped loop about one-third of the way down a piece of the cut wire. Before making the wrap, attach the loop to one of the bead dangles and to the open loop of the last link you made (figure 2).

fig. 2

6. String one bicone bead and make a wrapped loop on the other end of the wire to complete the link.

7. Repeat steps 5 and 6 to make nine or 10 more two-part links.

8. Repeat steps 3 to 7 to add strands to the second and third clasp loops. Work to keep all three strands the same length. Test for fit, keeping in mind that you will be adding one more link length to connect to the other half of the clasp. Adjust the strands as needed.

9. Slide the clasp halves together.

10. Add the last link to the end of the first strand, but this time work the second wrapped loop of the link so it attaches to a bead dangle and the coordinating loop on the other half of the clasp. Repeat for each strand.

summer nights

Brush up on your wire-wrapping skills with this charming project.
Its whites, purples, and blues recall cool summer nights, but you
can switch up the colors for any look you like.

Designer: Beki Haley

Finished Size: 7¼ inches (18.4 cm) long

Materials

Sterling silver chain-link bracelet

Assorted glass beads

Metal beads

Freshwater pearls

Assorted charms

22-gauge sterling silver head pins, 2 inches (5.1 cm)

22-gauge sterling silver open jump rings, 5 to 6 mm

22 teardrop silver puffy charms, 12 x 9 mm

Tools

Round-nose pliers

Flat-nose pliers

Wire cutters

Designer's Tip

Looking for a one-of-a-kind gift for someone special? Ask close friends to purchase a unique charm or two and present them in prettily wrapped packages. Afterward, bring all of the charms home and make them into a bracelet that will become a cherished keepsake.

Instructions

1. Select the beads and charms so that the colors and sizes work well together. Lay out your beads and charms and design the groupings that will go on each head pin. Design each one a little differently for a unique look.

2. Add some charms to the ends of some of the head pins by cutting off the head and making a loop in which to attach the charm. Twist your wire to make a nice professional loop.

3. Lay out your design to keep it uniform and balanced but not symmetrical. Attach your newly created charms to your bracelet with jump rings.

captured pearls

These bracelets use spool pegs to knit beads and wire together. Finished bracelets can be twisted in one direction to accentuate the spiral effect or twisted in both directions and then straightened to make the knitted loops appear thinner.

Designer: Barbara Van Buskirk

Finished size: 7¼ inches (18.4 cm) long

Materials

Spool of 24-gauge copper wire

Strand of freshwater pearls or semiprecious nuggets, 4–8 mm

Copper bracelet findings

2 copper jump rings

Tools

Wire cutters

Knitting spool (commercially purchased or homemade replica)

Steel crochet hook

Instructions

1. Thread the entire strand of beads onto the spool of wire. Do not cut the wire.

2. Drop about 6 inches (15.2 cm) of the wire down into the spool. Wind a loop around the first peg. Slide a bead between the first loop and the next peg (clockwise or counterclockwise, whichever is most comfortable for you).

3. Continue making loops and sliding beads as you work around the pegs until you're back at the first peg.

4. Make another loop on the first peg and bring the bottom loop over the peg with your crochet hook.

5. Repeat steps 3 and 4 until you're about an inch (2.5 cm) from your desired length. Tug on the length as it comes through the bottom of the spool when the peg area becomes too crowded.

6. Carefully lift the work off the pegs and slide it out of the spool. Cut the wire about 6 inches (15.2 cm) past the last bead. Take the working end of the wire and go through each loop at least once. (This step is the equivalent of casting off in knitting.)

7. Join a jump ring to each end of the bracelet using the wire as a sewing needle. Tuck in the wire ends and attach the findings.

bloodstone

A reddish form of chalcedony, carnelian is a stone that is found in royal
Sumerian bead cloaks, ancient Roman signet rings, and this classic bracelet.

Materials

Designer: Andrea L. Stern

Finished size: 8 inches (20.3 cm) long

1-foot (30.5 cm) length of 24-gauge sterling silver wire, or 5 silver head pins, each 3 inches long (7.6 cm)

8 matte coral seed beads, size 6/0

18 Chinese turquoise disks, 8 mm

8 brown ceramic disks, 8 mm

8 aqua white heart India glass barrel beads, 6 mm

Large carnelian or agate round bead, approximately 15 to 18 mm

Magnetic clasp

Tools

Ruler or tape measure

Round-nose pliers

Wire cutters

Designer's Tip

The magnetic clasp likes to grab onto any of the metal, which is why you want to put it on last in step 8.

Instructions

1. Use the round-nose pliers to make a loop at one end of the silver wire by bending it at a 90° angle, approximately ¼ inch (6 mm) from the end.

2. String a seed bead, a Chinese turquoise disk, a ceramic disk, a Chinese turquoise disk, and a seed bead onto the wire. Bend the wire at a 90° angle, and use the wire cutters to cut it approximately ¼ inch (6 mm) from the bend. Using the round-nose pliers, make a simple loop, closing it as close to the end bead as possible.

3. Make a loop at one end of the rest of the long piece of wire, but before closing it, attach the first piece so that it dangles from the end of the loop.

4. String a barrel bead, a Chinese turquoise disk, a ceramic disk, a Chinese turquoise disk, and a barrel bead onto the long piece of wire. Make a simple loop as in step 2.

5. Repeat steps 2 through 4 one time, attaching each new link to the link before it. You now have four links on your bracelet.

6. String a Chinese turquoise disk, the big carnelian bead, and a Chinese turquoise disk, and make a loop.

7. Now, alternate barrel bead/turquoise disk/ceramic disk/ turquoise disk/barrel bead links with the seed bead/turquoise disk/ceramic disk/ turquoise disk/seed bead links, attaching them in reverse order so that they're a mirror image of the links on the other side of the big carnelian bead link. You should have a total of nine links on your bracelet.

8. Open the loop at one end and slide the magnetic clasp on. Close the loop. Repeat on the other end.

9. If you choose to use head pins instead, simply make the loops in the same manner. You can expect to get about two links per head pin.

outrageous

Extravagant! Over the top! Use the largest crystals and craziest charms you can find to give this eye-catching piece its extreme personality.

Designer: Linda Larsen

Finished size: 7 inches (17.8 cm) long

Materials

10 sterling silver rondelle spacers, 4 mm

5 faceted round crystals, 18 mm

3 vintage round sterling silver balls with set crystals, 18 mm

5 freshwater rice pearls, 18 mm

7 sterling silver charms, 25 to 51 mm

10 sterling silver bead caps, 10 mm

22 sterling silver jump rings, 10 mm

Sterling silver toggle clasp

8 ball-end sterling silver head pins, 2½ inches (6.4 cm) long

16-inch (40.6 cm) length of 16-gauge sterling silver wire

6½-inch (16.5 cm) length of sterling silver chain, 13 mm

Scraps of chain to total 15 inches (38.1 cm), 2 mm

Tools

2 pairs of chain-nose pliers

Round-nose pliers

Flush wire cutters

Pencil

Instructions

1. Connect all of the charms, evenly distributed, to links on the oversize chain, using a jump ring for each one.

2. Slide a rondelle spacer, crystal, and rondelle spacer onto a ball-end head pin. Make a wrapped loop above the upper rondelle spacer. Open a jump ring and slip the loop onto it, attach the crystal on the first link of the oversize chain, and close the jump ring. Assemble and attach the remaining crystal dangles in the same manner, evenly spacing them along the chain.

3. Thread each of the silver balls with set crystals onto a ball-end head pin, and make a simple loop at the top (wrapping the wire twice around the tip of the round-nose pliers). Attach these dangles to the oversize chain using jump rings.

4. Cut three lengths of tiny chain: 1¼, 1, and ¾ inches (3.2, 2.5, and 1.9 cm). Cut a 3-inch (7.6 cm) length of wire. Make a simple loop at one end, using the round-nose pliers. Open it with the chain-nose pliers, add the end link of each piece of small chain, and then close the loop. Add a bead cap, a freshwater pearl, and another bead cap to the wire. Finish the top of the dangle with a wrapped loop. (You may have to ream out the pearl to get the wire through.) Make four more pearl dangles in the same manner.

5. Attach all of the pearl dangles to the oversize chain with jump rings, as shown in figure 1.

fig. 1

6. Attach the parts of the toggle clasp to the ends of the oversize chain, using jump rings.

golden dunes

Like a pearl spotted on a sandy beach, this bracelet
is an unexpected delight to keep and treasure.

Designer: Elizabeth Larsen

Finished size: 8 inches (20.3 cm) long

Materials

7-foot (2.1 m) length of 20-gauge full-hard or half-hard gold-filled wire

96 round strawberry conch shell beads, 5 mm

14 gold spacer rings

22-foot (6.7 m) length of 24-gauge (full-hard or half-hard) gold-filled wire

Cement adhesive for nonporous surfaces

10 coin golden-lip shells, 15 mm

19 coin brown-lip shells, 10 mm

9 medium freeform mother-of-pearl nuggets

Tools

Tape measure

Knitting needle (for jump rings), size 2 US (2.75 mm)

Wire cutters

2 pairs of needle-nose pliers

Round-nose pliers

Instructions

1. Make the base chain. First, create your own jump rings as follows. Cut a 6-foot length (1.8 m) of the 20-gauge gold-filled wire and wind it tightly in a coil around the knitting needle. (You'll need 118 jump rings altogether.) Slide the coil off the needle, and spread the rings slightly to make them easier to cut. Cut one ring off with the flush side of the wire cutters, then flip the cutters to cut the other wire tip of the ring flush. Continue with the other rings in the coil. Link the jump rings in pairs, using the two needle-nose pliers to make a 6½-inch (16.5 cm) chain. (Later you'll attach each half of the toggle clasp to the chain with the extra jump rings.)

2. Next, start to make the ring of the toggle clasp. Use the wire cutters to cut a 3½-inch (8.9 cm) piece of 20-gauge gold-filled wire, and then make a simple loop at one end with the round-nose pliers.

3. Add 11 of the round strawberry conch shell beads, with one gold spacer ring in between each shell. Curve the wire into a ring, making sure the beads are spaced far enough apart so that the wire can bend into a circle. Close with a second simple loop, and rotate the ends so they are parallel to each other. Connect the two ends together with a jump ring.

4. To make the bar of the clasp, measure and cut a 1¾-inch (4.4 cm) piece of 20-gauge gold-filled wire, and create a simple loop at one end. Add three conch shell beads and two gold spacers, interspersing the spacers between the beads.

Designer's Tip

If you would prefer not to make your own jump rings as described in step 1, you can instead go to a jewelry supply store or catalog and purchase 20-gauge gold-filled jump rings with an interior diameter of 3 mm or slightly less. If you do, you will only need a 1-foot (30.5 cm) length of gold-filled wire to make the project.

5. Take an extra piece of 20-gauge gold-filled wire and create a small figure eight (i.e., two simple loops). Add the figure eight to the toggle bar, and then slide three additional conch shell beads onto the bar, with gold spacers between them as in step 4. Close off the bar with another simple loop. Attach the figure eight to the end of the base chain with a jump ring (figure 1).

fig. 1

6. To prepare all of the beads for assembly, start by cutting a 2-inch (5.1 cm) to 2½-inch (6.4 cm) piece of 24-gauge gold-filled wire. (The larger shells may need the larger piece of wire.) Using the round-nose pliers, form a simple loop at one end. Add one of the beads to the wire. Secure the wire end and bead with a dab of glue. Repeat this step for each bead.

To construct the bracelet, lay out the beads in the following order:
- *3 strawberry conch shell beads
- Golden-lip shell
- Brown-lip shell
- Strawberry conch shells
- Mother-of-pearl nugget
- Brown-lip shell

Repeat from * with the remaining beads.

7. Start at one end of the chain, and begin attaching the beads. Attach one bead to either side of a link set, using the wrapped loop technique. Continue adding beads in this fashion until you come to the end of the bracelet. Adjust the beads on each link so that there are not too many of the same beads on one side.

whirlpool

Roll silver wire into spirals and curves that link and swirl around focal beads.

Designer: Tamara Honaman

Finished size: 8¾ inches (22.2 cm) long

Materials

Focal bead, 20 mm

6 round sterling silver beads, 3 mm

12 sterling silver rondelle spacers, 5 mm

4 lampwork glass beads, 8 to 10 mm

2 sterling silver charms, 10 to 15 mm

13 sterling silver jump rings, 6 to 10 mm

6 sterling silver ball-end head pins,
2½ inches (6.4 cm) long

34½-inch (87.6 cm) length of 14-gauge
sterling silver wire

24-inch (61 cm) length of 24-gauge
sterling silver wire

Tools

2 pairs of chain-nose pliers

Flat-nose pliers

Round-nose pliers

Heavy-duty flush wire cutters

Tape measure

Ball peen hammer

Instructions

1. Cut a 3-inch (7.6 cm) piece of 14-gauge wire with a blunt cut at both ends. Slightly flatten each end with a hammer. Grip the tip of the wire in the round-nose pliers. Rotate your wrist away from your body to form a ⅛ to ³⁄₁₆-inch (3 to 5 mm) eye at the end of the wire. Rotate the piece and make an eye at the other end, in the opposite direction.

2. Place the wire in the jaws of the round-nose pliers, near the hinge. Rest one eye just above the plier's barrel, and pivot, with the eye coming up, toward you. Rotate the pliers away from you to form a shepherd's hook. Repeat this motion at the opposite end of the wire to complete an S-link. Link a jump ring through both eyes. Make two more S-links.

3. Cut a 5-inch (12.7 cm) piece of 14-gauge wire with a blunt cut at both ends. Slightly flatten both ends with a hammer. Use the round-nose pliers to make an eye at the tip of the wire. Grip the eye and rotate your wrist again, wrapping the wire to start the second layer of the spiral.

4. Grip the growing spiral, flat in the flat-nose pliers, and lay wire down around the previous layer. Build the spiral—moving the wire while holding the pliers in one position—until 1 to 1½ inches (2.5 to 3.8 cm) of wire remain. Form a new eye at the end of the remaining wire. Grip the large spiral with the flat-nose pliers, grip the smaller loop with the chain-nose pliers, and then flip the smaller loop so it is vertical to the larger spiral. Change your grip on the eye and then continue wrapping the wire to start the second layer of a new spiral (figure 1).

fig. 1

5. Blunt-cut a 6-inch (15.2 cm) length of 14-gauge wire. Slightly flatten the ends. Make an eye at one end of the wire, and make a spiral no more than two revolutions deep. Tightly wrap the 24-gauge wire around 4 inches (10.2 cm) of the 14-gauge wire, and slide this up to the base of the small spiral, working the coil into the spiral so the coil is caught or stabilized. Trim any excess wire. Continue making the spiral, incorporating the coil, until you have 1 inch (2.5 cm) of 14-gauge wire remaining. Make a new eye, in the opposite direction to the first spiral, at the remaining end of the 14-gauge wire. Continue to spiral the wire until it meets the previous spiral.

6. Blunt-cut a 4½-inch (11.4 cm) piece of 14-gauge wire. Make an eye at one end, and then work a spiral until 2 inches (5.1 cm) remain. Using the round-nose pliers, grip the wire above the spiral. Bend the remaining length of wire around one barrel of the pliers to form the neck of the clasp (figure 2). Grip the tip of the wire, and form an eye to finish the end of the swan clasp. With the hammer, slightly flatten the curve of the neck.

fig. 2

7. To start the first half of the focal bead cage, measure the outside of the focal bead, from hole to hole. Add 4 inches (10.2 cm). Cut a piece of the 14-gauge wire to this final measurement. Blunt-cut both ends of the wire. Shape the wire into a spiral at one end that is large enough to span the hole of the focal bead.

8. Place the spiral over a hole on the focal bead. Bend the wire over the bead, to the hole on the other side. The amount of wire past the hole should be just enough to make a spiral. Create the second spiral, curling it in the opposite direction.

9. Place the spiral piece of the cage around the focal bead. Blunt-cut a 4-inch (10.2 cm) length of 14-gauge wire. Insert the wire through the hole in the center of one spiral, through the focal bead, and out the center of the second spiral. Center the focal bead on the wire.

10. Bend the wire to cross at one end of the bead. Make spirals at each end of the wire until the holes meet. Keep the spirals loose enough to allow enough space for the focal bead to move smoothly.

11. Add a rondelle spacer, lampwork glass bead, rondelle spacer, and small round bead onto a head pin. Make a wrapped loop just above the stacked items, threading the dangle onto the last jump ring in the linked items. Make five more dangles, using the beads, charms, and head pins. Slip two dangles onto one curve of two of the S-shaped wire pieces.

12. Making sure that the finished piece is relatively flat so it can rest horizontally on a flat surface, link the elements together, using jump rings as needed (figure 3). Attach the remaining dangles to jump rings that have been used to link the shaped wire pieces. Attach the swan clasp to one end.

fig. 3

gardens of babylon

A handful of brass bugle beads form the 10 shimmery strands of this French-inspired piece.

Designer: Kaari Meng

Finished size: 6¼ inches (15.9 cm) long

Materials

165 silver glass bugle beads, 2 x 5 mm

1-inch (2.5 cm) length of brass cable chain, 6 mm

2 brass 5-ring connectors, 22 mm

80 brass eye pins, 1 inch (2.5 cm)

6 brass head pins, 1 inch (2.5 cm)

11 brass jump rings, 3 mm

2 brass jump rings, 5 mm

Brass spring ring clasp, 12 mm

Tools

Needle-nose pliers

Wire cutters

Instructions

1. Thread two bugle beads onto each eye pin. Loop eight eye pins together to form one strand, making 10 strands total.

2. Attach a 3-mm jump ring to two strands and then attach to the bracelet connector. Repeat on the opposite end of the strand.

3. Connect the chain to one end of the connector using a 5-mm jump ring. Thread the head pins with the bugle beads; cut and loop. Gather all five head pins onto a 3-mm jump ring; connect to the end of the chain. Attach the clasp to the opposite end of the bracelet using a 5-mm jump ring.

savored souvenirs

The designer of this bracelet searches for souvenir penny machines everywhere he travels. These charming machines flatten and imprint a penny with a specially engraved die.

Designer: Terry Taylor

Finished size: 8 inches (20.3 cm) long

Materials

10 teardrop beads, 13 mm

15 flat souvenir pennies

10 head pins, 2 inches (5 cm) long

17 copper jump rings, 5 mm

Copper toggle clasp

15-inch (38.1 cm) length of copper link chain, 5 mm

Teaspoon of salt

¼ cup white vinegar

Tools

2 pairs of chain-nose pliers

Needle-nose pliers

Wire cutters

Rawhide mallet

Shallow glass bowl

Hand towel

Awl or nail with a flat head

Safety glasses

Drill and ¹⁄₁₆-inch (1.6 mm) drill bit

Half-round file

Instructions

1. Souvenir pennies may be slightly curved when they come out of the machine. If this is the case, place them on a sturdy work surface, one at a time, and tap on them with a rawhide mallet to flatten them.

2. Pour the salt and vinegar into the bowl. Stir the mix until the salt is dissolved. Place the pennies in the bowl to soak for about five minutes. When removed, wipe the pennies with a hand towel to reveal the shiny surface.

3. Use an awl or nail to make a divot at the top of the penny, where you wish to drill a hole (figure 1). Use a small drill bit to create a hole in each penny. Smooth the edges with the file.

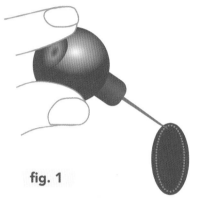

fig. 1

4. Cut the chain into two equal lengths. Spread both pieces in front of you. Plan the finished position of the pennies and beads by placing them underneath the chains. Leave these items in position as you work through the next few steps.

5. Attach pennies to the chain links of both lengths of chain, using a jump ring for each penny.

Designer's Tip

You can purchase flattened pennies online, but that's not as much fun as finding a machine or imprinting your own.

If you don't have a rawhide mallet, sandwich a penny between two pieces of scrap wood and flatten the penny with a regular hammer.

6. Slide a bead onto a head pin. Roll the head pin to create a loop. Slide the wire through a chain link (figure 2). Wrap the end of the wire around the head pin that is coming out the top of the bead. Cut off the excess wire. Attach all of the remaining beads to both chain lengths in the same manner.

fig. 2

7. Open a jump ring and slip on part of the toggle clasp and the last link of one end of each chain. Close the jump ring. Use another jump ring to attach the remaining toggle clasp part and the opposite ends of the chains.

grand tour

This piece includes a potpourri of beads from all over the world. Just imagine it's a record of the items you've collected along your journeys.

Designer: Jean Campbell

Finished size: 9¾ inches (24.8 cm) long

Materials

5 grams of root beer seed beads, size 11/0

Antiqued brass button with shank, 1 inch (2.5 cm)

2 gold-filled crimp tubes, 2 x 2 mm

White bone wide-holed spacer, 2 x 9 mm

8-inch (20.3 cm) antiqued brass chain, 2 x 4 mm

13 carnelian spacer beads, 4 x 6 mm

Brown, black, and metallic gold lampworked glass long oval bead, 9 x 25 mm

4 burnt-orange dyed-bone coin beads with designs, 5 x 16 mm

45 African copper heishi beads, 3.5 mm

2 Bali-style vermeil spacers, 5 x 8 mm

3 gold quartz teardrops with front-to-back hole, 12 x 18 mm

Brown, black, and metallic gold lampworked glass cube, 12 mm

2 white bone barrels, 6 x 12 mm

8-inch (20.3 cm) length of shiny brass decorative chain, 3 x 4 mm

2 white bone barrels, 6 x 12 mm

10 carnelian melons, 6 mm

10 shiny brass melons, 3 mm

10 gold-filled head pins, 2 inches (5.1 cm) long

Tools

Ruler or tape measure

Wire cutters

Crimping pliers

Bead stop

Chain-nose pliers

Round-nose pliers

Instructions

1. Cut a 20-inch (50.8 cm) length of beading wire with the wire cutters. String on approximately 47 seed beads or enough to fit snugly around the antiqued brass button. (These seed beads will form the loop that holds the toggle of the button to close the bracelet.) Slide the beads to the center of the wire. Gather the wire ends together, and string one crimp tube through both wires. Snug the beads, and use the crimping pliers to crimp the tube.

2. With the wire ends still gathered, string the bone spacer and slide it over the crimp tube.

3. On one end of the wire, string beads as follows:
   • Three seed beads
   • An end link on the antiqued brass chain
   • One carnelian spacer
   • Lampworked oval
   • One carnelian spacer
   • Four seed beads
   Then snug the beads.

5. Again, stretch the antiqued brass chain along the beads just strung, and pass the wire through the closest link. Now string beads in the following order:
   • One seed bead
   • One carnelian spacer
   • Four seed beads
   • Lampworked cube
   • Four seed beads
   • One heishi
   • One carnelian spacer followed by one heishi, a total of three times
   • Three seed beads

6. Stretch the antiqued brass chain and pass the wire through the closest link. String in the following order:
   • Three seed beads
   • One coin
   • Five seed beads
   Pass the wire through the antiqued brass chain's open end link. Place the bead stop on the wire to hold the beads.

7. On the other end of the wire, string in the following order:
   • Four seed beads
   • An end link of the shiny brass chain
   • Two seed beads
   • Two heishi
   • One carnelian spacer
   • Two heishi
   • Two seed beads
   • One coin
   • Four seed beads
   • Three heishi
   • One carnelian spacer
   • One teardrop
   • One carnelian spacer
   • Three heishi
   • Three seed beads

4. Stretch the antiqued brass chain alongside the beads just strung, and pass the wire through the closest link (figure 1). Next, string beads as follows:
   • Three seed beads
   • One coin
   • Seven seed beads
   • Three heishi
   • One vermeil spacer
   • One carnelian spacer
   • One teardrop
   • One carnelian spacer
   • One vermeil spacer
   • Three heishi
   • Eight seed beads

fig. 1

8. Stretch the shiny brass chain along the beads just strung and pass the wire through the closest link. Next string in the following order:
   - Five seed beads
   - One bone barrel
   - Five heishi
   - One carnelian spacer
   - Four heishi
   - Three seed beads

9. Stretch the shiny brass chain and pass the wire through the closest link. String in the following order:
   - Two seed beads
   - One coin
   - Three seed beads
   - Five heishi
   - One carnelian spacer
   - Four heishi
   - One teardrop
   - Three heishi
   - Three seed beads

10. Stretch the shiny brass chain and pass through the closest link. String in the following order:
    - Two seed beads
    - Two heishi
    - One bone barrel
    - Two heishi
    - Three seed beads

11. Stretch the shiny brass chain and pass through the closest link. String six seed beads.

12. Remove the bead stop from the other wire end. Gather the wire ends together and string one crimp tube and the button. Pass both wires back through the crimp tube, snug all the beads, and crimp.

13. Slide one carnelian melon and one brass melon on a head pin. Use the chain-nose and the round-nose pliers to form a wrapped loop that attaches to the fifth link of the brass chain. Repeat the process until you've evenly placed a total of 10 carnelian dangles down the length of brass chain.

orient
express

Turn your travel memories into jewelry with this eclectic charm bracelet. Anything will work—from game pieces to old coins.

Designer: Candie Cooper

Finished size: 7½ inches (19 cm) long

Materials

Focal beads and pendants, up to 20 mm

Bead assortment, 4 to 20 mm

2 base metal picture frame charms, 17 mm

Base metal charms, 25 to 44 mm

Base metal head pin for each focal bead,
2 inches (5.1 cm) long

Base metal eye pin for each charm,
2 inches (5.1 cm) long

Toggle clasp

Base metal jump rings, 5 mm

Base metal jump ring for charms and
dangle, 5 mm

7-inch (17.8 cm) length of base
metal chain, 10 mm

2 pieces of silk fabric, newspaper, or
ticket stubs to fit the picture frame charms

Chinese replica coin with center hole,
25 mm

6-inch (15.2 cm) length of silk cord

Game pieces and coins, 22 to 26 mm

1 bead for each game piece, 5 mm

Craft glue

(continued on page 86)

(continued on page 86)

Instructions

1. Slide interesting pieces of fabric, newspaper, or ticket stubs into the picture frames. Connect these to the chain with a jump ring.

2. Thread the cord through the hole in the coin. Wrap one end around the coin and through the hole again. Add a jump ring and tie the cord ends in a knot (figure 1). Use this jump ring to connect the coin to the chain.

fig. 1

3. Continue making pieces, one for each chain link, and arranging them below the chain as they are completed. Do not attach any more until all of the pieces are finished. This will help you establish attractive spacing between the pieces, as well as ensure that pieces look nice next to each other.

4. For coins that need to be drilled, make the hole less than ¹⁄₁₆ inch (1.6 mm) from an edge.

5. Drill ½ inch (1.3 cm) into the top of each game piece. Thread a 5-mm bead onto a 2-inch (5.1 cm) piece of wire. Make a simple loop at the end. Trim the wire so the loop butts against the game piece when the wire is inserted in the drilled hole. Dip the end of the wire into the glue, and then insert the wire into the hole (figure 2).

fig. 2

Tools

2 pairs of chain-nose pliers

Flat-nose pliers

Round-nose pliers

Wire cutters

Ruler

Scissors

Safety glasses

Drill and #55 drill bit (optional)

Center punch and hammer

320-grit sandpaper

6. Thread each focal bead onto a head pin, and finish with a simple loop or wrapped loop. Place a small charm in the loop of an eye pin, and close the loop. String one to three beads onto the pin, and finish with a simple loop at the top. To make a bead dangle, thread an accent bead onto an eye pin, and finish with a simple loop.

7. Connect the toggle clasp to the ends of the chain with 5-mm jump rings. Attach each piece to the bracelet.

spiral axis

Individually, the spiral dangles in this project appear somewhat plain, but fill a handmade chain with them and you end up with a stunning piece that's runway worthy.

Designer: Elizabeth Larsen

Finished size: 8¼ inches (21 cm) long

Materials

24 lavender half-round potato freshwater pearls,
5 mm to 6 mm

13 purple oval freshwater pearls, 5 to 6 mm

76 violet crystal rounds, 6 mm

15 light amethyst crystal rounds, 6 mm

Sterling silver and marcasite toggle clasp, 19 mm

5-foot (1.5 m) length of 20-gauge, full- or half-hard
sterling silver wire

32-foot (9.8 m) length of 24-gauge, full- or half-hard
sterling silver wire

Jeweler's cement adhesive

Tools

Flush cutters

Flat-nose pliers

Chain-nose pliers

Round-nose pliers

Knitting needle, 2.75 mm (size 2 US)

Instructions

Note: The materials are for a 6¾- to 7-inch (17.2 to 17.9 cm) wrist. Add or subtract materials to make a larger or smaller bracelet.

1. Tightly coil the 20-gauge wire around the knitting needle down the needle's length. Slide the end of the coil off the end of the needle. Cut the coils one at a time to make jump rings. Make 130 jump rings in all.

2. Open two jump rings. Connect the two rings to two closed (stacked) jump rings. Repeat to make a chain 64 links long (figure 1).

fig. 1

   You should have two jump rings left over. Use one to connect one half of the clasp to one end of the chain. Repeat at the other end. Set the chain aside.

3. Cut a 3-inch (7.6 cm) piece of 24-gauge wire. Form a wrapped loop at one end of the wire. String on a pearl and form a second wrapped loop, but don't cut the wire.

4. Hold the second loop with a pair of flat-nose pliers. Use chain-nose pliers to wrap the wire around and down the body of the bead until the wire meets the first loop. Loosely wrap the wire end around the first loop's base, and use chain-nose pliers to tighten the wrap (figure 2). Secure the wire end by adding a dab of adhesive where you've made the wrap. Repeat with each bead to make a total of 128 dangles. Set them aside.

fig. 2

5. Lay the dangles on the work surface in the following sequence: one lavender pearl, four violet crystals, one light amethyst crystal, one lavender pearl, two violet crystals, and one purple pearl. Repeat the sequence until you've arranged all the dangles.

6. Carefully open the second set of links at one end of the bracelet without dismantling the chain. Attach the first lavender pearl dangle. Slide the links around so they open at the other side of the chain and attach the next dangle in the sequence from step 5 (the first violet crystal). You should end up with one dangle on each side of the chain (figure 3).

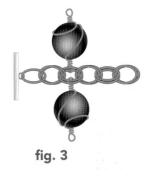

fig. 3

7. Continue to add dangles down the length of the chain, following the sequence from step 5, until you reach the other end. The placement of dangles may be adjusted so there aren't too many of one kind of bead on one side of the bracelet.

wandering gypsy

Eclectic, colorful, energetic—this bracelet's carefree mix of texture
and bright shapes is just as fun to put together as it is to wear.

Designer: Diane Guelzow

Finished size: 8¼ inches (21 cm) long

Materials

42 assorted beads (pearls, crystal, sterling silver, glass, polymer clay, bone, round and donut-shaped semiprecious stones, and large seed beads)

20-inch (45.7 cm) length of 16-gauge sterling silver wire for the links and the hook

15-inch (38.1 cm) length of 18-gauge brass wire for the jump rings

10-inch (25.4 cm) length of 20-gauge sterling silver wire for the eye pins

9 sterling silver head pins, 4 mm

Tools

Chasing hammer

Steel bench block

Dowel, ½ inch (1.3 cm) in diameter

Instructions

1. Cut the 16-gauge silver wire into six pieces, each 2½ inches (6.4 cm) long; set aside the 2-inch (5.1 cm) piece that's left. File the ends smooth. Using the chasing hammer and working on a steel bench block, flatten the last ⅛ inch (3 mm) of the wire ends slightly.

2. With round-nose pliers, form side loops, facing in opposite directions, on the wire ends (see figure 1). Form each piece of wire into an S to create a link (see figure 2).

fig. 1   **fig. 2**

3. To give the links some variety, gently hammer the outermost parts of the loops on the bench block. If the hammering distorts their shapes, reshape them with round-nose pliers. Set the links aside.

4. Using the dowel and the 18-gauge brass wire, make 15 jump rings. Hammer them slightly, but if their ends spread apart a bit as a result, reshape them as needed.

5. To assemble the bracelet, connect the links with two jump rings between each. Add a single jump ring to one of the outer links to serve as part of the closing clasp. Set aside the remaining two jump rings.

6. Create the hook for closing the bracelet with the leftover piece of 16-gauge wire from step 1. File both ends smooth. Gently hammer the last ⅛ inch (3 mm) of the ends flat. Using round-nose pliers, create a small side loop on one end. Shape this side of the wire into a hook, then flatten all but the loops. On the other end of the wire, create a large side loop, bending it perpendicular to the hook. Use two jump rings to attach this loop to the last link.

7. Make three jump rings of any diameter you like out of the brass wire and at least 15 eye pins from the 20-gauge wire, some with creatively shaped bead stops, such as spirals and wrapped loops. Slip between one and three beads on each of these, as well as on the purchased head pins. Trim and file the eye and head pins as needed. Attach beads to all of the links and the jump rings between them.

talisman

Repetition of shapes unifies a quirky assortment
of metal plates and found objects.

Designer: Susan Lenart Kazmer

Finished size: 7 inches (17.8 cm) long

Materials

Dark-color beads, 5 to 8 mm

Tube of dark-color 11° seed beads

Brass, copper, sterling silver, or stainless steel rectangular found objects, 10 x 25 mm to 9 x 40 mm

Brass, copper, and stainless steel circular found objects, 10 to 30 mm

22-gauge sterling silver sheet metal

Jump rings in various metals, 5 to 8 mm

Ball-end sterling silver head pins, 2 inches (5 cm) long

Sterling silver eye pins, 2 inches (5 cm) long

Sterling silver clasp

24-gauge base metal wire

16-gauge annealed steel wire

6½-inch (16.5 cm) length of base metal chain, 6 mm

Antiquing, liver of sulphur, or patina solution

Matte medium

Paper printed with images and words, to fit the found objects

Thin sheet of mica or clear, hard plastic

(Continued on page 94)

Instructions

1. Cut the sheet metal into rectangles ranging from ⅜ to ⅝ inch (1 to 1.6 cm) wide and 1 to 2 inches (2.5 to 5.1 cm) long. Cut several pairs to the same size. Use the metal file to clean up and smooth the edges by pushing the file away from you. Oxidize or apply the antiquing or patina solution to the rectangles. Glue very small scraps of paper to some of the pieces with the matte medium. Set aside the matching rectangles for use in step 2.

2. Select two scraps of paper to showcase between two matching pieces of flat metal. Draw a rectangle with a fine-tip permanent marker where you want to cut out a window that will allow you to see the paper inside when the riveting is finished. Drill a hole in a corner of the window. Insert the blade of the jeweler's saw into the hole and fix the other end into the saw. Saw along the drawn lines until the center falls out. Use the metal file to clean up and smooth the edges by pushing the file away from you. Make a matching window in the other piece of metal.

3. Cut two pieces of mica or clear, hard plastic, both slightly larger than the window. Place the mica under each window, with a paper image on top.

4. Stack all the layers (silver sheet metal, mica, paper image (face down), paper image (face up), mica, and silver sheet metal) with the metal edges aligned (figure 1). Place the stack in a small clamp. Drill straight through all the layers at a corner.

fig. 1

Tools

Designer's Tip

Rivets are the strongest method of attaching metal to metal besides soldering. For a piece that has unusual materials, such as wood, paper, and plastic, you don't have the option of soldering since these materials wouldn't survive the heat.

5. Place the stack on an anvil. Insert the already filed annealed wire all the way into the hole. This should be a tight fit. Place the flush wire flat against the top sheet. Raise the cutters just less than ⅜ inch (1 cm) above the sheet metal, and snip off the wire (figure 2). Do not move the stack. Using a very small ball peen hammer, tap gently around the outside of the extended wire until the top starts to look like a nail head.

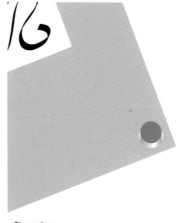

fig. 2

6. Gently turn over the stack, and work the other side in the same manner. Once your first rivet is complete, there will be less shifting and you can then drill the rest of the holes. Work all of the holes in the same manner, and file them so they are smooth and clean. Make at least four rivets in a small piece, and then check for buckling. You may need to add another two to four rivets. Complete as many window rectangles as desired.

7. Smaller items could be lost amid the larger pieces. The solution is to combine several small objects as a single dangle. For example, thread a seed bead onto a 2-inch (5.1 cm) ball-end head pin, and then stack several small metal disks and washers on top. Finish with a simple loop. Combine items on head pins to create dangles.

8. As necessary, drill holes at the top and bottom of items, attach a piece of 24-gauge base metal wire, and then roll a loop for each hole.

9. The effect of this bracelet is created by using mostly long pieces, combining several smaller found objects to create a longer dangle, and by using many pivot points. Make links by combining several pieces on an eye pin, and then rolling a simple loop at the top. Now you can use a jump ring to attach the top of a smaller, metal rectangle to the bottom of the link. Small springs that you find inside some pens make excellent links: Unwind the very top and bottom of the spring, and wrap each of the ends around jump rings (figure 3).

fig. 3

10. Continue building dangles. You need enough to attach at least one dangle on each side of every link in the bracelet chain. As you work, consider using wrapped loops, rather than simple loops, at the top of some dangles. Simple loops are the easiest, but a triangular wrap will allow a drop bead to move. This will add more visual texture to your finished piece.

11. Use jump rings to attach the clasp to the chain, and then attach the dangles to the chain, again using jump rings.

mime

Designer: Marty Stevens-Heebner and Christine Calla

Finished size: 8½ inches (21.6 cm) in circumference

Materials

60-inch (1.5 m) length of 18-gauge sterling silver wire

3 large black buttons with 2 holes apiece, or flat beads with large center holes

3 large clear buttons with 2 holes apiece, or flat beads with large center holes

3 large white buttons with 2 holes apiece, or flat beads with large center holes

Tools

Craft scissors

Wire cutters

2 pairs of round-nose pliers

This bracelet is inspired by the black-and-white costumes of Marcel Marceau, Charlie Chaplin, Pierrot, and other pantomimes. The curves and the color scheme echo the jaunty grace of the classic clowns.

Instructions

1. Cut a 20-inch (50.8 cm) piece of the 18-gauge wire, fold the wire in half, and create a loop at the center. Then twist the wire sides together beneath this loop two to three times.

2. Cut a 40-inch (1 m) piece of the 18-gauge wire, and thread this wire through the loop made in step 1 until the loop rests at the center of the 40-inch (1 m) wire. Then fold the 40-inch (1 m) wire in half inside the loop and draw it down next to the wires leading from the loop.

3. There should now be a total of four lengths of wire leading from the loop: the two shorter lengths of wire from step 1 and the two longer lengths from step 2. Wrap one of the longest lengths of wire tightly around the other wires four to six times, then bring the four lengths together again, side by side.

4. Slide a large black button onto the two longest lengths of wire, about 1 inch from where the wire was wrapped in step 3. Add a clear button and a white button. Allow the two shortest lengths of wire to pass beneath the buttons, then use the needle-nose pliers and your fingertips to wrap the wire ends in a spiral pattern on top of the ring four to six times.

5. Now draw the longest wire from the top down and around the buttons in the direction of the wire loop. Wrap this wire three to five times around all four lengths of wire, next to the button. Now pull this wire beneath the buttons so that it joins the two shortest lengths.

Designer's Tip

The length of wire required for this project may vary according to the size of your wrist.

6. Draw the other wire from the top around the buttons, away from the wire loop made in step 1. Wrap this wire three to five times around all four lengths of wire on the opposite side of the buttons. Then straighten the wire so that it joins the other three lengths.

7. Repeat steps 4 through 6 two additional times, this time adding the buttons ¾ to 1¼ inches (1.9 to 3.2 cm) from where the wire was wrapped in step 6, depending on the desired size of the bracelet.

8. Fold the longest remaining piece of wire in half approximately 1¾ to 2¼ inches (4.4 to 5.7 cm) from the last wire wrapping, depending on the desired size. Bend this wire ¼ to ½ inch (6 mm to 1.3 cm) from the top around the round-nose pliers to form a hook. Wrap this wire two to three times around the others, then trim away any excess wire. Then wrap each remaining wire two times around the other wires to secure the bracelet together. Trim each piece with the wire cutters, then wrap the next length of wire on top of the cut to disguise it.

afternoon bazaar

Stunning medleys of African beads are separated by
silver spacers from Thailand.

Designer: Sherry Duquet

Finished size: 8 inches (20.3 cm) long

Materials

10-inch (24.4 cm) length of 0.014-inch
(0.4 mm) flexible beading wire

13 mixed African trade beads, ranging from
8 to 25 mm

2 sterling silver round finishing beads, 3 mm

2 sterling silver crimp tubes, 2 x 2 mm

2 sterling silver crimp covers, 3 mm

7 sterling silver rondelles, 4 mm

Sterling silver toggle clasp, 15-mm circle,
24-mm bar

Tools

Beading board

Ruler or tape measure

Crimping pliers

Flat-nose pliers

Nonsticky silicone plastic putty (optional)

Instructions

1. On the beading board, plan out a design using 13
   mixed African trade beads interspersed with five
   sterling silver rondelles. String the beads one at a time
   onto the beading wire. Finish by placing one sterling
   silver rondelle, a 3-mm silver finishing bead, and a
   crimp tube on each end. You can place the putty on
   one end to hold beads in place.

2. Take one end of the toggle clasp and thread the
   beading wire through the hole. Feed the beading wire
   back through the crimp tube, 3-mm finishing bead,
   silver rondelle, and one African bead, hiding the wire
   end in the bead. Use the crimping pliers to crimp the
   crimping tube firmly around wire. Remove the putty
   from the opposite end.

3. Take the other end of the toggle clasp, pull the wire
   through snugly, and repeat step 2.

4. Before crimping the second end, pull the wire firmly,
   but not too tightly, then crimp and trim any excess
   wire. Use the flat-nose pliers to close 3-mm crimp
   covers around the crimp tubes on both sides.

Designer's Tip

Silicone plastic putty is a great tool to keep the
beads on one end from sliding off while crimping
the opposite end. It doesn't stick to the wire or
to the beads.

blue cloisonné

Both the French and the Russians are known for their cloisonné beads. No matter what the era, these traditional enamel beads always seems to be in fashion.

Designer: Marty Stevens-Heebner and Christine Calla
Finished size: 8½ inches (21.6 cm) long

Materials

Tigertail wire
10 Indian sapphire crystal bicone beads, 6 mm
10 bead caps
3 cloisonné beads, 22 x 15 mm
5 pale blue crystal bicone beads, 4 mm
2 cloisonné beads, 30 x 20 mm
2 crimp beads
Jump ring
Clasp

Tools

Craft scissors
Wire cutters
2 round-nose pliers

Instructions

1. Cut a 13-inch (33 cm) piece of the tigertail wire, then string an Indian sapphire bead onto the wire, followed by a bead cap, a 22 x 15-mm cloisonné bead, a second bead cap, an Indian sapphire bead, and a pale blue crystal bicone bead. Repeat this beading pattern, this time using a 30 x 20-mm cloisonné bead.

2. Repeat the entire beading pattern from step 1. Then repeat the first part of the beading pattern. Once you've added the pale blue crystal bead, add a crimp bead to both ends of the wire.

3. Thread one wire end through the jump ring, then back through the crimp bead and the first crystal bead. Pull the wire until it's tight, then crush the crimp bead, and trim any excess wire. Repeat the crimping process on the opposite side of the bracelet, this time substituting the clasp for the jump ring.

fairy garden

A thing of beauty can also be simple. Cavorting fairies and a rainbow of precious crystals are attached using jump rings and simple loops.

Designer: Marlynn McNutt

Finished size: 7½ inches (19 cm) long

Materials

6 bicone crystals in capri blue, green, light purple, light yellow, pale brown, and red, 8 mm

5 top-drilled polygon crystals in brown, burgundy, light purple, pale blue, and purple, 13 mm

2 top-drilled AB polygon crystals, 13 mm

2 sterling silver dragonfly charms, 20 mm

Sterling silver dragonfly charm, 14 mm

3 sterling silver fairy charms, 17, 18, and 20 mm

Sterling silver moon goddess, 16 mm

6 sterling silver head pins, 1½ inches (3.8 cm) long

14 sterling silver jump rings, 6.5 mm

Clasp

Tools

Chain-nose pliers

Needle threader

Ruler

Scissors

Glue

Instructions

1. Insert a head pin into each of the bicones, and make a simple loop at the top of every one.

2. Twist open all of the jump rings.

3. Slip a large dragonfly charm onto a jump ring and then insert the jump ring through the first link of the bracelet at the clasp end. Close the jump ring. Attach an AB polygon to the next link of the bracelet in the same manner.

4. Threading jump rings to the charms and polygons and opening the simple loop at the top of each bicone, continue adding crystals and charms to the bracelet. Skip links for attractive spacing, and place the dangles in the following order: the capri blue bicone, largest fairy, purple polygon, light purple bicone, small dragonfly, pale blue polygon, light yellow bicone, moon goddess, brown polygon, green bicone, 17-mm fairy, light purple polygon, red bicone, remaining fairy, burgundy polygon, pale brown bicone, large dragonfly, and AB polygon (figure 1).

fig. 1

Designer: Patty Cox

Finished size: 9 inches (22.9 cm) long

Materials

60-inch (1.5 m) length of 26-gauge silver wire

2 silver crimp beads, size 2

4 mint green cat's eye round beads, 6 mm

6 oval pearls, 3 mm x 6 mm

5 crystal bicone faceted beads, 4 mm

Crystal rainbow seed beads

Silver spring ring clasp

Tools

Needle-nose pliers

Jig

Nylon-jaw pliers

Wire cutters

cat's eye

Gleaming cat's eye beads and pearls are framed with tiny crystal seed beads and alternated with filigree-framed crystal bicones.

Instructions

1. Cut three 18-inch (45.7 cm) lengths of wire. Thread a crimp bead, then one side of the spring ring clasp on all three wires. Fold the wires over the clasp ring. Slide the crimp bead next to clasp over all the wires. Crimp the bead.

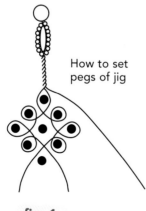

How to set pegs of jig

fig. 1

2. Thread a 4-mm cat's eye bead over all the wires. Cut the short wire tails.

3. Separate the three wires. Thread an oval pearl on the center wire. Thread eight seed beads on each outer wire. Pull all the beads tightly toward the clasp end. Twist the wires ¼ inch (6 mm).

4. Place the pegs in the jig according to figure 1. Loop each outer wire around the pegs. Remove from the jig. Flatten the wire loops with the nylon-jaw pliers. Option: Pinch with your fingertips.

5. Bring the center wire back to the center. Thread with a crystal bicone.

6. Following the wire filigree with the bicone, twist all three wires together ¼ inch (6 mm).

7. Separate the three wires. Thread a cat's eye on the center wire. Thread eight seed beads on each outer wire. Pull all the beads tightly. Twist the wires ¼ inch (6 mm).

8. Continue adding the pearls, filigree, and cat's eye beads to make a bracelet 9 inches (22.9 cm) long.

9. Attach the other half of the clasp at the end of the wires. Try on the bracelet and adjust as needed. Slide a crimp bead over all the wires and crimp to secure. Trim the ends.

tickled
pink

Feminine and funky, the bold beads and delicate bows
in this piece will tickle the fancy of anyone who loves pink.

tickled pink

Designer: Tair Parnes

Finished size: 7½ inches (19 cm) long

Materials

25–30 large glass beads, various shapes and shades of pink

5 pink satin bows

25–30 silver eye pins

19 silver jump rings, ¼ inch (6 mm)

2 silver 6-strand connector bars

Fabric glue

Two-part silver clasp

Tools

Wire cutters

Round-nose pliers

2 pairs of flat-nose pliers

Instructions

1. String a bead onto an eye pin. Make a loop and trim any excess wire. Repeat to string all of the beads onto eye pins (photo 1).

photo 1

2. Attach a jump ring to each satin bow. Add a dab of fabric glue to secure the jump ring in place (photo 2).

photo 2

3. Attach jump rings to the six loops on one of the connector bars.

4. String a bead onto two adjacent jump rings on the connector bar. Repeat to attach three beads to the six jump rings (photo 3).

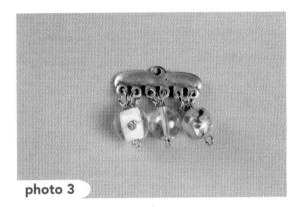

photo 3

5. Attach a bead to each of the beads you attached in step 4.

6. Continue connecting beads in this manner until the bracelet is the right length. The beads are different sizes, so make sure that all three chains are the same length.

7. Attach two jump rings onto the last bead in each chain. Attach each jump ring to one of the six loops on the other connector bar.

8. Attach the bows to the chains in a random fashion.

9. To finish, attach jump rings to the single loop on each of the connector bars and attach the clasp.

A Bounty of Bead & Wire Bracelets 105

celtic crystal

Pairs of double-spiral elements in this design recall the intricacies of a Celtic motif. Combined with crystal beads, the result is a wonderfully wearable bracelet.

Designer: Marie Lee Carter

Finished size: 8½ inches (21.6 cm) long

Materials

6 rondelle beads,* 6 mm diameter

14-inch (35.6 cm) length of 16-gauge sterling silver wire, for the spiraled elements

15-inch (38.1 cm) length of 20-gauge sterling silver wire, for the bead links

7 sterling silver 16-gauge jump rings, 6 mm

10 to 12 sterling silver 16-gauge jump rings, 4.5 mm

* The holes must be large enough to accommodate 20-gauge round wire.

Tools

Hammer and block

Round-nose pliers

Wire cutters

Instructions

1. Make the double-spiraled elements by cutting six pieces of 16-gauge wire, each 2 inches (5.1 cm) long. Flatten each end by striking it three or four times with a hammer. Make pairs of symmetrical spirals on each. Set aside.

2. Put on protective eyewear. Make a chain of three linked wrapped-loop beads with the 20-gauge wire. Repeat.

3. To make the hook, use the remaining 2-inch (5.1 cm) piece of 16-gauge wire. Make a large hook with a tiny loop at one end and a larger loop at the other. File any rough edges, then gently hammer the hook's curve.

4. Join pairs of double-spiraled elements by lining one atop the other and inserting a 6-mm jump ring through the centers of both. File any burrs. Lay open each pair, as you would a book, with the coils to the inside.

5. Connect the double-spiral elements with 4.5-mm jump rings.

6. Use a jump ring to connect the ends of the double-spiral linked chain to an end loop of a trio you made in step 2.

7. To make the clasp's eye, attach a 6-mm jump ring to one end of the bracelet; using a 4.5-mm jump ring, attach the hook to the other. (You may use additional jump rings to extend the length of the bracelet.) File any burrs.

shimmer & shake

The irresistible iridescence of the dichroic glass paired with small crystal beads will create movement certain to catch someone's eye.

Designer: Nancy Kugel

Finished size: 8½ inches (21.6 cm) long

Materials

4 rectangular dichroic segments, each approximately ¾ inch (1.9 cm) long, with loops at both ends

2 dichroic segments, each approximately ⅝ inch (1.6 cm) long, with single loops

4 fire-polished rondelles in a coordinating color, 6 mm

8 silver hill tribe bead caps

56 crystal bicones, 4 mm

48 silver head pins

6 silver head pins

20-inch (50.8 cm) length of 22-gauge silver wire

Silver toggle clasp

Jump rings

Ear wires of preference

Tools

Wire cutters

Round-nose pliers

Instructions

1. Lay out your beads. Using the wire cutters, cut four lengths of wire, each long enough to accommodate stringing two bead caps, a 6-mm rondelle, and the making of wrapped loops at both ends.

2. String the beads as shown, then use the round-nose pliers to make wrapped loops for attaching them to the dichroic segments. Attach one side of the toggle clasp to each end. You may need to attach a few jump rings to the bar side of the toggle in order to make the clasp close easily.

3. String the crystal beads on the head pins and attach four to each loop on the dichroic segments using either wrapped or simple loops.

apple
blossoms

This bracelet recalls the festive glass manufactured
during the 1930s. The reds and yellows blend
together with some help from the green glass leaves.

Designer: Kaari Meng

Finished size: 8 inches (20.3 cm) long

Materials

7½-inch (19 cm) length of brass chain

5 glass apples embedded with wire

2 brass bezels, 8 mm

3 brass bezels, 14 x 14 mm

2 garnet cabochons, 8 mm

3 jonquil glass cabochons, 12 x 12 mm

2 brass flowers

5 red glass flowers

4 yellow glass flowers embedded with wire

20 brass head pins, 1 inch (2.5 cm)

Brass jump ring, 8 mm

7 brass jump rings, 3 mm

6 red glass ladybugs

10 green glass leaves

Brass spring ring clasp, 12 mm

Tools

Jeweler's glue

Needle-nose pliers

Wire cutters

Instructions

1. Glue the jonquil and garnet cabochons onto the bezels; set aside to dry.

2. Cut the glass apples and glass flowers embedded with wire; loop directly onto the chain every third link. Thread the ladybugs, leaves, and red flowers onto head pins; cut and loop directly onto the chain on every other link. Connect the brass flowers onto the chain with the 3-mm jump rings.

3. When the cabochons have finished drying, open a 3-mm jump ring and attach to the chain. Note: Use these cabochons as fill-in pieces and sprinkle throughout bracelet where needed.

4. Attach the clasp to one end of the chain using the remaining 3-mm jump ring. Open the 8-mm jump ring and attach it to the opposite end of the chain.

Designers: Marty Stevens-Heebner and Christine Calla

Finished size: 8 inches (20.3 cm) long

Materials

40-inch (1 m) length of tigertail wire

87 freshwater pearls, 4 mm

8 spacer bars, each with 3 holes

26 red crystal bicone beads, 4 mm

6 crimp beads

Clasp

Jump ring

Silver chain for bracelet extender (optional)

Headpin for bracelet extender (optional)

Tools

Craft scissors

Wire cutters

Pliers

ladder of pearls

Lustrous freshwater pearls paired with brilliant red crystal beads make this piece timeless.

Designer's Tip

You can use either a jump ring or an end spacer to join the ends of the bracelet together. Either design works—it's just a matter of personal taste.

Instructions

1. Cut three 10-inch (25.4 cm) lengths of the tigertail wire.

2. Slide one of the pearls onto a piece of the wire, then thread the wire through the top hole of one of the spacer bars. Add four pearls and one of the crystal beads to the strand, then thread the wire through the top hole of the second spacer bar. String a crystal bead and four pearls onto the strand and add a spacer bar. Repeat this pattern two more times, making sure to thread the wire through the top hole of the spacer bar each time.

3. Thread four pearls and a crystal bead onto the strand, followed by the sixth spacer bar and another crystal bead to complete the pattern. This strand should be approximately 6 inches (15.2 cm) long.

4. Repeat steps 2 and 3 with another piece of the tigertail wire, but thread the strand through the hole on the opposite side of the spacer bars, making sure to leave the middle hole empty for now.

5. Begin the third strand of the bracelet by sliding a crystal bead onto it, then thread the wire through the center hole of the first spacer bar.

6. String a crystal bead onto the strand followed by four pearls and a spacer bar, again threading the wire through the center hole. Now add four pearls, a crystal bead, and the third spacer bar. Repeat this pattern two more times.

7. For the last segment of the bracelet, string a crystal bead and four pearls onto the strand, slip the wire through the final spacer bar, then add a pearl to finish the strand. Lay the three strands down next to each other on a flat surface and slide one of the crimp beads onto each end of the pieces of wire.

8. Take one end of the first strand and thread the wire through the jump ring attached to the clasp. Then thread it back through the crimp bead and the first crystal bead. Pull the end of the wire until the crimp bead butts up against the jump ring, then crimp the bead and trim away any excess wire.

9. Repeat step 8 with the opposite end of the strand, using the jump ring and making sure the wire is pulled tightly enough so that no gaps remain between the beads. Then repeat steps 8 and 9 with the two other strands to finish the bracelet.

10. If desired, make a bracelet extender by cutting a 1-inch (2.5 cm) piece of the silver chain with the wire cutters. Use the needle-nose pliers to open the jump ring from step 9, then slip one end of the chain onto the jump ring and close the ring.

11. To complete the extender, slide a crystal bead onto the headpin. Grasp the end with the round-nose pliers, and wrap the wire around one prong of the pliers to form a small loop. Slide this loop through the remaining end of the silver chain. Wrap any remaining wire around the pin between the bottom of the loop and the top of the bead using the needle-nose pliers.

santa fe cuff

The pairing of both
linear and circular forms
gives this cuff a unique look,
and the turquoise lends it a
Southwestern touch.

Designer: Michaelanne Hall

Finished size: 8 inches
(20.3 cm) in circumference

Materials

5 gold-filled round beads, 4 mm
in diameter

24 turquoise round beads, 4 mm in
diameter

31-inch (78.7 cm) length of 20-gauge
half-hard sterling silver square wire
for the cuff's exterior and the hook

26-inch (66 cm) length of 20-gauge
half-hard 14-karat gold-filled square
wire for the cuff's interior

6½-inch (16.5 cm) length of 24-gauge
half-hard 14-karat gold-filled square
wire for stringing the beads

46-inch (1.2 m) length of 20-gauge
half-hard 14-karat gold-filled half-
round wire for the wraps (38.1 cm),
2 mm

Tools

Masking tape

Instructions

1. Straighten the silver wire, then cut
    one piece 15½ inches (39.4 cm) long
    and two pieces each 6½ inches (16.5
    cm) long. Mark the center of the long
    piece with a permanent marker, center
    it in the jaws of the flat-nose pliers,
    and bend both sides of the wire to
    make a U. Set aside these wires.

2. Cut the 20-gauge gold-filled square
    wire into four pieces, each 6½
    inches (16.5 cm) long. Mark ½
    inch (1.3 cm) from each end.

Use a pin vise to twist all four
pieces of wire between the marks,
leaving the ends untwisted.

3. String all the beads on the
    24-gauge wire, alternating four
    turquoise beads with a gold one.

4. Place the U-shaped silver wire
    from step 1 on your work surface;
    its legs will be the outermost wire
    of the cuff. Place all the 6½-inch
    (16.5 cm) wires between the
    legs and parallel to each other,
    alternating the twisted wires with
    the silver ones; put the beaded
    wire in the middle. Align the ends
    of the seven straight wires ¼ inch
    (6 mm) away from the U-shaped
    bend. Use masking tape to secure
    all the wires on each end, keeping
    the square wires flat.

5. Mark the interior wires at their
    midpoints. Center the third gold bead
    from the end on this midpoint mark.

6. Cut 10 pieces of 20-gauge half-round
    wire, each 3 inches (7.6 cm) long. Use
    needle-nose pliers to make a hook at
    one end of each piece.

7. Working directly next to the center
    gold bead, hook the sharp bend of
    one of the half-round wires over
    the silver outermost wire and,
    using needle-nose pliers, make
    three wraps around the bundle
    of wires. Trim it and finish by
    hooking the end to the inside.

8. Slide four turquoise beads against the
    wire wrap you just made and, using
    the same method as before, wrap a
    piece of half-round wire on the other

side of the beads to frame them. Slide
one gold bead against this wrap, then
wrap another piece of half-round wire
on the bead's other side. Repeat, leaving
the last four turquoise beads on this
side free. Repeat with the beads on the
other side of the center gold bead.

9. Cut two pieces of half-round wire,
    each 18 inches (45.7 cm) long.
    Hook one piece next to the last set
    of four turquoise beads closest to the
    U-shaped bend in the silver wire.
    Wrap the half-round wire 16 to 18
    times, until the ends of the interior
    parallel wires are no longer visible.
    Repeat on the other side, leaving the
    two outermost silver wires exposed.

10. Use flat-nose pliers to bend the
    outermost silver wires outward 45°.
    Trim each to ⅜ inch (1 cm) long. Use
    round-nose pliers to roll them inward
    to make loops.

11. To make the hook for the clasp, cut a
    piece of square silver wire 2½ inches
    (6.4 cm) long. Bend it into a
    U shape. Using round-nose pliers held
    perpendicular to the wire, grasp the
    tip of the bend and angle it slightly.
    To form the hook, move your pliers
    to just beyond the angled tip and use
    your fingers to bend the wire ends
    around the outer part of the tool's
    tip. Now bend the ends of the wire
    outward 30°. Mark ⅜ inch (1 cm)
    from each end and make a loop from
    that length of wire. Attach the hooks
    to the loops on the cuff.

12. Starting at the middle of the bracelet,
    slowly and gently shape its form until
    you can close the clasp.

paris

A chain brought back from the City of Light inspired this bauble.
To enhance the memory, charms nestle among crystals salvaged
from an old chandelier.

Materials

Designer: Carol McGoogan

Finished size: 7½ inches (19 cm) long

6 top- and bottom-drilled chandelier crystals, 17 mm

6 silver-filled star charms, 5 mm

3 photo frame charms, 18 mm

22 Paris-themed charms: gold, brass, nickel, copper, and silver-filled, 6 to 13 mm

24 brass jump rings, 4 mm

12 brass head pins (optional, see step 1), 2 inches (5.1 cm) long

Toggle clasp

7-inch (17.8 cm) length of antiqued brass chain, 4 to 6 mm

3 pictures to fit the frame charms

Clear craft lacquer

Clear-drying all-purpose glue stick

Tools

2 pairs of chain-nose pliers

Flat-nose pliers

Round-nose pliers

Wire cutters

Scissors

Paintbrush (if the lacquer does not include an applicator)

Instructions

1. Spread the chain in front of you and place the crystals, evenly spaced, along the length of the chain. To attach these, use the wire that connected each crystal to the chandelier. These wire pieces are ideal because each one already has a nice brad on the end. If you do not have the original wire (or are using new crystals), use head pins instead. Insert the wire or head pin, from front to back, through the top hole in the crystal. Trim the wire so it is just long enough to roll a loop over the end of the round-nose pliers. Once the simple loop is formed, the crystal can be attached to the chain using a jump ring.

2. Attach a miniature star to the hole in the bottom of each crystal, again using the original chandelier wire or a head pin (figure 1).

3. Cut an image to fit inside each of the frame charms. Using the glue stick, attach the image to the frame. Cover the image with clear craft lacquer, letting the lacquer seep over the edges of the image and onto the metal surface.

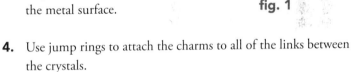

fig. 1

4. Use jump rings to attach the charms to all of the links between the crystals.

5. Use a jump ring at each end of the chain to attach the parts of the toggle clasp.

Designer's Tips

Remove the links from the leftover bracelet chain to make perfectly matched jump rings.

Do not shake the bottle of clear craft lacquer, as this will create bubbles you will not be able to remove when you coat your photos. Also, always let this lacquer dry completely, preferably overnight, before handling the piece.

You can never have too many charms!

caged beads

Wire cages are a beautiful way to show off your spectacular beads. For added variety, try experimenting by caging some of the beads with twisted wire or making cages in different shapes.

Designer: Mami Laher

Finished size: 8 inches (20.3 cm) long

Materials

12-foot (10.8 m) length of 18- or 20-gauge round wire for cages

5 or more oval beads, 10 x 13 mm, or round beads, 10 mm, with openings large enough for 18-gauge wire to fit through

3-foot (2.7 m) length of 18-gauge round wire for center pins and jump rings

6 metal beads, 8 mm

Clasp

Tools

Round-nose pliers

Chain-nose pliers

Flush cutters

Instructions

1. For each caged bead, cut a 9-inch (2.3 cm) length of 18- or 20-gauge round wire. Make loops at both ends of the wire, holding the wire ⅓ of the way into the mouth of the round-nose pliers.

2. Using flat-nose pliers, coil the wire halfway from each end to form a symmetrical, S-shaped scroll. Hold the middle of the scroll with the pliers and bend the top half of the scroll onto the bottom half so that the two halves are stacked.

3. Grab the center of one of the coils with the flat-nose pliers and pull gently, stretching the coil out about ⅜ inch (1 cm). Repeat with the other coil in the opposite direction.

4. Pry the cage open slightly where the gap between the wires is widest and insert an oval bead. Close the gap by bending the wires back into place.

5. Repeat steps 1–4 to make the remaining cages. Note: This bracelet measures 8 inches (20.3 cm) and uses five caged beads. For extra length, simply add an additional caged bead.

6. Cut a 1¾-inch (4.4 cm) length of 18-gauge wire for each cage and insert through the center of the caged bead. Make loops at each end of the cage from the protruding wire by bending the wire at a 45° angle (or slightly more) and then grabbing the wire end with pliers and bending to complete the loop.

7. Thread each metal bead onto a 1¼-inch (3.2 cm) length of 18-gauge wire. Make loops at one end of the bead from the protruding wire as you did in the end of step 6.

8. Connect the caged bead units to the metal accent beads and close the loops with pliers. Attach clasp findings to finish.

seed bead bangles

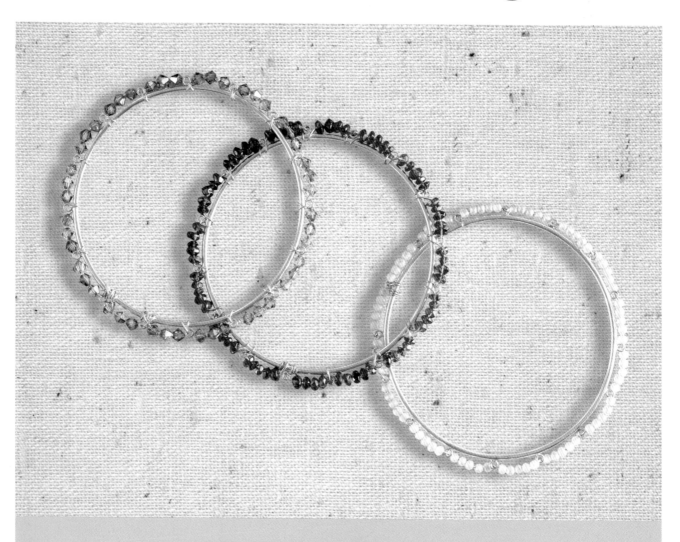

These gold-plated bangles are studded with colorful
seed beads, lending a playful edge to an elegant piece.

Designer: Kaari Meng

Finished size: 8 inches
(20.3 cm) in circumference

Materials

3 gold-plated bangles

80 garnet chips, 3 mm

80 glass pearl seed beads, 2 mm

48 tourmaline crystals, 3 x 5 mm

3-yard (2.7 m) length of 24-gauge
gold-plated wire

Tools

Needle-nose pliers

Wire cutters

Instructions

1. Cut the wire to 1 yard (91.4 cm). Wrap the end of the wire twice around a bangle loop to secure. Wrap the wire around the bangle once and then thread five garnet chips onto the wire. Wrap again through the loop on the bangle and then around the bangle once. Continue attaching five garnets at a time between each loop.

2. Repeat the above steps to complete the pearl and tourmaline bangles. When threading the pearl seed beads onto the bangle, thread five onto the wire between each loop. Thread three tourmaline crystals between each loop. Once all beads are wrapped onto the bracelet, wrap the wire around the bangle two more times.

Designer's Tip

This bracelet is made using a gold-plated bangle that has small (2 mm) rings soldered to the outside of the bangle. You can use any size seed bead to change the look of the bracelet, or simply attach beads with a jump ring to each loop to create a beaded dangle look.

wire links

Add as many dangles as you wish to the undulating curves of this freeform wire bracelet.

Designer: Tamara L. Honaman

Finished size: 7¼ inches (18.4 cm) long

Materials

4 top-drilled sapphire AB crystal heart beads, 10 mm

1 top-drilled crystal AB crystal crescent bead, 20 mm

6 sapphire crystal bicone beads, 8 mm

12 crystal AB crystal helix beads, 8 mm

3 top-drilled aqua crystal baroque pendants, 16 x 11 mm

36 sterling silver round beads, 2.5 mm

36 sterling silver daisy spacer beads, 5 mm

4 sterling silver spiral charms with loop, 7 x 10 mm

4 silver-plated pinch bails

18 sterling silver head pins, 2 inches (5.1 cm)

12 sterling silver 20-gauge jump rings, 5.5 mm

16 sterling silver jump rings, 8 mm

30-inch (76.2 cm) length of 14-gauge dead-soft sterling silver wire

Tools

Wire cutters

Round-nose pliers

Chain-nose pliers

Flat-nose pliers

Hammer

Steel block

Instructions

Making the Links

1. Cut a 3-inch (7.6 cm) piece of wire. Hammer the last ¼ inch (6 mm) of the wire on the steel block. Repeat for the other end.

2. Grasp one end of the wire with the tip of the round-nose pliers. Rotate your wrist to form a small loop. Repeat on the other end of the wire, so each has a loop facing the same direction (figure 1).

fig. 1

3. Grasp the center of the wire with the largest part of the round-nose pliers' jaws. Bend the wire until the two small loops meet, making a U shape (figure 2).

fig. 2

4. Use round-nose pliers to grasp one side of the wire ¼ to ½ inch (6 mm to 1.3 cm) below the bend you just made. Rotate your wrist so the wire end bends downward. Repeat for the other half of the wire to create an M-shaped link (figure 3).

fig. 3

5. Repeat steps 1 through 4 to create seven or eight more links, depending on the length you want for your bracelet. Set aside.

Variation

Making the Clasp Eye

1. Cut a 1-inch (2.5 cm) piece of wire. Hammer the last ¼ to ½ inch (6 mm to 1.3 cm) of the wire on the steel block. Repeat for the other end.

2. Grasp one end of the wire about ¾ of the way down the round-nose pliers' jaws. Rotate your wrist away from you until the wire touches itself, creating a large loop.

3. Grasp the other end of the wire with the tip of the round-nose pliers and rotate your wrist away from you until the wire touches itself, creating a small loop that goes in the opposite direction (figure 4). Set aside.

fig. 4

Making the Clasp Hook

1. Cut a 2-inch piece of wire. Hammer the last ¼ to ½ inch (6 mm to 1.3 cm) of the wire on the steel block. Repeat for the other end.

2. Grasp one end of the wire near the tip of the pliers. Rotate your wrist away from you until the wire touches itself, creating a small loop.

3. Grasp the wire about ½ to ¾ inch (1.3 cm to 1.9 cm) above the loop you just created with the largest part of the round-nose pliers' jaws, and bend the

fig. 5

wire until it meets the small loop you just made. Grasp the other end of the wire near the tip of the round-nose pliers, and bend the wire in the opposite direction from the last bend until the wire touches itself, creating a small decorative loop. Hammer the hooked portion of this piece, if desired (figure 5). Set aside.

Connecting the Links

1. Lay out the links on the work surface so the first link is positioned like an M, the following one like a W, the next like an M, etc.

2. Open the large jump rings. Connect the first two links together using two jump rings. Close the jump rings (figure 6). Repeat until all the links are connected.

![fig. 6 illustration of connected links]

fig. 6

3. Use two jump rings to attach the hook half of the clasp to the small loop on one end of the bracelet. Close the jump rings. Use chain-nose pliers to open the end loop on the other end of the bracelet and attach the eye half of the clasp. Close the loop.

Creating the Dangles

1. String one round bead, one spacer bead, one bicone bead, one spacer bead, and one round bead onto one head pin. Begin a wrapped loop. Before completing the wrap, attach the loop to a bend on the first link of the bracelet. Complete the wrap (figure 7). Trim any excess wire and use chain-nose pliers to tuck in the wire end.

fig. 7

2. String one round bead, one spacer bead, one helix bead, one spacer bead, and one round bead onto one head pin. As in step 1, make a wrapped loop that attaches to the same bend you embellished in step 1.

3. Continue making dangles following steps 1 and 2, and add them along the length of the bracelet as you go. Note: You'll want to add all of the dangles in the following steps to the same side of the bracelet so they hang properly when worn.

4. Open a small jump ring and connect it to a baroque bead. Attach it to a link on the bracelet and close the jump ring. Repeat to add the remaining baroque beads so they are evenly spaced down the length of the bracelet.

5. Open a bail and connect it to a heart bead. Close the bail. Open a small jump ring and connect it to the bail's loop. Attach the jump ring to a link on the bracelet and close the jump ring. Repeat to add the remaining heart beads so they are evenly spaced down the length of the bracelet.

6. Open a small jump ring and connect it to a charm. Attach it to a link on the bracelet and close the jump ring. Repeat to add the remaining charms so they are evenly spaced down the length of the bracelet.

7. Open a small jump ring and connect it to the crescent bead. Attach it to a link at the end of the bracelet and close the jump ring.

figure eight

The figure-eight wire links that form the backbones of these bracelets create strong, durable pieces of jewelry. Although these bracelets were made with the same technique, their individual looks come from the variations in the bead links.

Designer: Gary Helwig

Finished size: 8 inches (20.3 cm) long

Materials

30-inch (76.2 cm) length of 22-gauge wire, plus extra wire for practice links

5 medium-size beads or 10 smaller-size beads

Clasp findings

Tools

Wire cutters

Round-nose pliers

Jig

Designer's Tip

You can create different looks by changing the space between pegs and/or changing the wire gauge—just have enough extra materials on hand to allow for several practice links

Instructions

1. Cut the wire into ten 3-inch (7.6 cm) lengths.

2. Make five bead links by forming a loop with one length of wire around the round-nose pliers, then sliding the bead down against the loop and making a second loop close to the bead. Trim any excess wire. Set the bead links aside.

3. To make a figure-eight link, position two large jig pegs ¼ to 3/16 inch (5 mm) apart. Tightly wrap a length of wire around the pegs in a figure-eight shape, leaving a ¾-inch (1.9 cm) tail at each end of the wire. Remove the figure eight from the jig by grasping it at the center point with round-nosed pliers. Repeat step 3 four more times.

4. Connect the bead links to the figure-eight links by slipping the bead links' loops onto the loops in the figure eights.

5. Finish the figure-eight links by bending the wire tails so they are perpendicular to the link. Hold the link in the middle with round-nose pliers and wrap the wire tails around the piece as shown in the illustration. Note that the wire from the right-hand loop forms the left-hand wrap around the center of the link, while the wire from the left-hand loop forms the right-hand wrap.

6. Place the bracelet on the intended wearer's arm and see if additional links are necessary.

7. Add the clasp findings.

fall charms

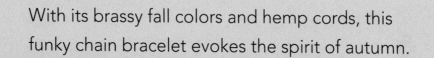

With its brassy fall colors and hemp cords, this funky chain bracelet evokes the spirit of autumn.

Designer: Erin Prais-Hintz

Finished size: 8 inches (20.3 cm) long

Materials

Lumber toggle and lumber links

2 brass jump rings, 16 gauge, each 12 mm

Brass jump ring, 16 gauge, 15 mm

4 brass jump rings, 16 gauge, each 9 mm

8 etched brass jump rings, 16 gauge, each 9 mm

Brass jump ring, 16 gauge, 6 mm

6 red jasper rectangular brick beads, each 12 mm

6 bronze round wires, 20 gauge, each 2 inches (5.1 cm)

36-inch (91.5 cm) length of cotton, hemp, or waxed linen cord

3 brass eye pins, 22 gauge, each 1½ inches (3.8 cm)

3 glass flower beads, each 5 mm

Tools

Round-nose pliers

Instructions

1. Cut a length of cotton hemp cord or natural colored string 10 to 12 inches (25.4 to 30.5 cm) long. Hold one end against a 15-mm plain brass jump ring, and start wrapping the cord tightly around the ring. When you have wrapped the cord completely around the ring with no gaps, securely tie the cord in an overhand knot. Trim the ends, leaving tails of about ½ inch (1.3 cm). Repeat this step for the two remaining 12-mm plain brass jump rings.

2. Using round-nose pliers, make a wrapped loop on one end of a 2-inch (5.1 cm) length of bronze wire. Thread a jasper rectangular bead onto the wire, and make a wrapped loop on the other end. Repeat this step for the remaining five rectangular brick beads.

3. Open all remaining jump rings.

4. Connect the bracelet in the following order, closing the jump rings as you go:
    Lumber toggle
    9-mm etched jump ring
    Cord-wrapped jump ring
    9-mm etched jump ring
    9-mm plain jump ring
    3 beaded links
    9-mm plain jump ring
    9-mm etched jump ring
    Lumber link
    9-mm etched jump ring
    Cord-wrapped jump ring
    9-mm etched jump ring
    9-mm plain jump ring
    3 beaded links
    9-mm plain jump ring
    9-mm etched jump ring
    Lumber link
    9-mm etched jump ring
    Cord-wrapped jump ring
    9-mm etched jump ring
    6-mm plain jump ring
    Toggle bar closure

5. Using brass eye pins, make a wrapped-loop dangle for each glass flower bead. Connect two flower beads to one 9-mm plain jump ring in the center of the bracelet. Add one flower bead to another 9-mm plain jump ring.

boho hand wrap

You'll feel exotic when you wear this sparkling hand wrap. For fun variations, oxidize the silver for more impact or add a chain extension to make a choker.

Materials

Designer: Jackie Guerra

Finished size: 7¾ inches (19.7 cm) long

17 Austrian crystal rosettes with three loops, 11 mm

44 Austrian bicone crystals to match, 4 mm

Austrian crystal briolette, 6 x 11 mm

5-inch (12.7 cm) length of silver chain

70-inch (1.8 m) length of 24-gauge sterling silver half-hard wire

Silver lobster clasp, 5 x 10 mm

2 silver jump rings, 3 mm

2 silver head pins

Oxidizing solution

Tools

Round-nose pliers

Flat-nose pliers

Flush wire cutters

Instructions

1. Cut 44 pieces of silver wire to 1½-inch (3.8 cm) lengths. (Silver eye pins the same length can be substituted when wire-wrapping the crystals.)

Designer's Tip

For a bracelet like this, pick a clasp that's easy to manipulate with one hand. A lobster clasp works well. Test it before buying!

2. Patina all the silver.

3. Arrange the rosettes on a flat surface with eight in the top row, five in the second row, four in the third row, and one in the last row. Alternate the directions of the rosettes in the top row so that the "triangles" of the three loops rotate—two on top, one on top, etc, across the row—so the rest of the bracelet will drape beautifully on the hand.

4. Attach the top row of rosettes across the top and the bottom with a wire-wrapped crystal between each rosette.

5. For the second row, attach the wire-wrapped crystals to the top two loops of each rosette and space them across, attaching them to the loops on the rosettes above.

6. For the third row, repeat with four rosettes with their two loops on the top. Attach wire-wrapped crystals to each of the top loops and connect them to the bottom loops of the second row.

7. Attach the last rosette with wire-wrapped crystals to the center two rosettes in the third row.

8. Using the head pins, dangle a crystal from the bottom loop of the two end rosettes in the second row.

9. Attach a wire-wrapped crystal from the bottom of the rosette in the fourth row.

10. With a longer piece of wire, wrap a hanger for the briolette. Create a loop at the top large enough to fit into the bottom loop of the wire-wrapped crystal in step 9 and two more wire-wrapped crystals (to be formed in step 11).

11. Cut a 3-inch length of chain, and attach two wire-wrapped crystals to each end. Attach the two ends of the chain and crystals to the top loop of the hanging briolette. This loop of wire will fit over a finger to hold the hand wrap in place.

12. Attach the lobster clasp to the last loop on the top row of rosettes on one side. On the other side, attach the remaining chain to the loop of the rosette with one last wire-wrapped crystal. Install the jump ring on the end of the chain.

stargazer

If you get starry-eyed over mystical dichroic-blue beads, you'll love making this adjustable bracelet. Tiny Bali spacer beads perfectly echo the wire's coil pattern.

Designer: Hanni Yothers

Finished size: 8½ inches (21.6 cm) in circumference

Materials

2 lampworked glass beads, 12 x 11 mm

5 lampworked glass beads, 7 x 11 mm

3 lampworked glass beads, 5 x 9 mm in diameter

5 Bali silver spacer beads, 1 x 6 mm in diameter

10-inch (25.4 cm) length of 12-gauge dead-soft sterling silver wire

24-inch (61 cm) length 18-gauge half-hard sterling silver wire

Tools

Steel wool

Cookie sheet

Instructions

1. Straighten the length of 12-gauge wire by working it gently with your fingers or pulling a soft cloth down the length of the wire while holding one end.

2. Hold the 18-gauge wire tightly crosswise to the 12-gauge wire, with a ½-inch (1.3 cm) tail. Coil the 18-gauge wire around the heavier wire, keeping your turns as tight as possible. Pull off the coil, which should be about 2½ inches (6.4 cm) long, and cut it into four ½-inch (1.3 cm) sections and two ¼-inch (6 mm) sections.

3. File one end of the 12-gauge wire, grasp it with pliers, and wind it loosely around them to make a flat spiral ½ inch (1.3 cm) in diameter. Try to get the curved spiral to touch the flat wire that leads to the bracelet to keep beads from moving onto the spiral.

4. Slide one of the ¼-inch (6 mm) coils onto the 12-gauge wire and push it up against the spiral. Add one of the 7 x 11-mm beads, a spacer, and a 5 x 9-mm bead. Add the following elements, in this order: ½-inch (1.3 cm) coil, 7 x 11-mm bead, spacer, 12 x 11-mm bead, ½-inch (1.3 cm) coil, 5 x 9-mm bead, spacer, 7 x 11-mm bead, ½-inch (1.3 cm) coil, 12 x 11-mm bead, spacer, 7 x 11-mm bead, ½-inch (1.3 cm) coil, 7 x 11-mm bead, spacer, 5 x 9-mm bead, and a ¼-inch (6 mm) coil.

5. Trim the 12-gauge wire so that 1½ inches (3.8 cm) extend beyond the last coil. File the sharp ends of the wire. Grasp the very end of the wire with pliers and spiral it in toward the beads until it touches the last coil you added to the bracelet, making sure that this spiral is on the same plane but facing in the opposite direction as the first spiral. The spiral should be tight up against the end of the ¼-inch (6 mm) coil so that the coil can't move onto the spiral.

6. Use your fingers to gently bend the bracelet into a shape that is comfortable to wear on your wrist, keeping in mind that the spirals should be flat against the underside of your wrist.

7. When you have a comfortable shape, put the bracelet on a cookie sheet and place it in your oven at 550°F (287.8°C) for 2 to 2½ hours; the heat will harden the sterling and make it more springy.

8. Remove the oxidation caused by the heat by brushing the bracelet with steel wool under running water until you achieve the desired finish.

squares & twists

Here's just an inkling of the incredible design possibilities of beads and wire. Varying the jig designs, the type of wire, and the beads can create an endless number of designs.

Designer: Lilli Johnson

Finished size: 7¾ inches (19.7 cm) long

Materials

For black bead bracelet

92-inch (2.4 m) length of 24-gauge colored wire

7 jump rings, 6 mm

Clasp findings

Tools

Wire cutters

Round-nose pliers

Pin vise

Jig

Flat-nose pliers

Instructions for the black bead bracelet

1. Cut the wire into two 46-inch (1.2 m) lengths. Place the ends in a pin vise and twist to create the desired effect. Cut the twisted wire into seven 6½-inch (16.5 cm) lengths.

2. Arrange the jig according to the pattern in figure 1. Place the center of the wire at the start peg and make loops 1, 2, 3, and 4. Slide the beads onto each end of the wire, then make loops 5, 6, 7, and 8.

3. Attach the links together with jump rings, then add clasp findings.

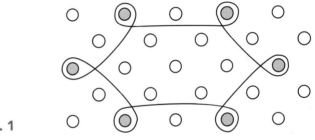

fig. 1

Materials

For blue bead bracelet

19 tube beads, 10 mm

86-inch (2.2 m) length of black wire

Clasp findings

Tools

Wire cutters

Jig

Small nail

Flat-nose pliers

Instructions for the blue bead bracelet

1. Cut the wire into 19 3½-inch (8.9 cm) lengths, two 2½-inch (6.4 cm) lengths, and one 14-inch (36 cm) length.

2. Arrange the jig according to the pattern in figure 2. Working with a piece of 3½-inch (8.9 cm) wire, make the first two loops, then slide on a bead and finish the second two loops. Repeat with the remaining 3½-inch (8.9 cm) lengths of wire.

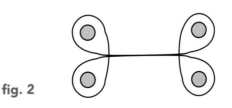

fig. 2

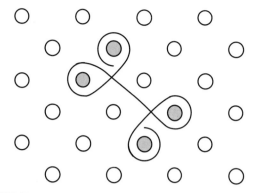

fig. 3

3. Arrange the jig according to the pattern in figure 3 and make two links from the 2½-inch (6.4 cm) wire.

4. Wrap the 14-inch (35.6) cm length of wire tightly arund the nail. Slide off the coil and cut down the middle to form jump rings. (You will need 42.)

5. Assemble the bracelet by attaching the outer loops of the bead links with jump rings on both sides. Attach one link made in step 3 to each end with jump rings, then use another jump ring to attach a clasp finding to the center loops.

Materials

For purple bead bracelet

16-inch (40.6 cm) length of 22-gauge gray wire

7½-inch (19 cm) length of 20-gauge silver wire

42 square beads, 4 mm

3 jump rings, 4 mm

Clasp findings

Tools

Wire cutters

Round-nose pliers

Jig

Instructions for the purple bead bracelet

1. Cut the gray wire into seven 2¼-inch (5.7 cm) lengths. Form a small loop on one end of a length of wire. Slide on three beads, then cross the wires over each other to form another loop in the center. Slide on three more beads and finish with a loop at the end. Trim off any excess wire.

2. Repeat step 1 six times. Curve each wire so that the looped ends are on top of each other and shape into a circle.

3. Cut six 1¼-inch (3.2 cm) lengths from the silver wire and use the pliers to form figure-eight shapes by bending one end in a loop toward the middle from the right and the other end in a loop toward the middle from the left. Leave a small gap in the loops.

4. Attach the links by sliding the bead link loops in the figure-eight link loops. Note: One side of the bead links will have two loops (from the ends); be sure to get both loops in the figure-eight link.

5. Add a jump ring to each end of the bracelet, and then add the clasp findings. Tighten any loose areas with pliers.

tropical charms

With its cowrie shells and turquoise seed beads,
this bright, funky piece looks both beachy and fun.

Designer: Tair Parnes

Finished size: 8 inches (20.3 cm) long

Materials

11 turquoise seed beads, size 6°

11 large beads, glass, plastic or stone, various sizes and shades of turquoise

3 cowrie shell beads

Silver leaf pendant, ¾ inch (1.9 cm) in length

Heart outline pendant

50 turquoise seed beads, size 11°

Tube bead, ¼ inch (6 mm) in length

6 small heart pendants, ¼ inch (6 mm) in length

11 head pins

3 eye pins

24 silver jump rings, ¼ inch (6 mm) in diameter

5 pairs of silver bead caps, sized to fit the large beads

Beading thread

2 pieces of 8-inch (20.3 cm) long, thick silver chain

Silver clasp

Tools

Round-nose pliers

Wire cutters

2 pairs of flat-nose pliers

Scissors

Beading needle

Instructions

1. To make a dangling charm, string a size 6° seed bead onto a head pin. Make a loop in the head pin and trim any excess wire. Repeat to make six decorated head pins.

2. String a large bead onto an eye pin. Make a loop in the eye pin and trim any excess wire. Attach the beads from step 1 to one of the loops and attach a jump ring to the other loop (photo 1).

3. To make a heart charm, attach a jump ring to the heart outline pendant. Attach a second jump ring to the first jump ring.

4. To make a simple bead charm, string a size 6° seed bead and one of the large beads onto a head pin. Make a loop in the head pin and trim any excess wire. Attach a jump ring to the loop. Repeat to make five simple bead charms.

5. To make a cradled bead charm, string a pair of bead caps and a large bead onto a head pin so that the bead caps cradle the bead. Make a loop in the head pin and trim any excess wire. Attach a jump ring to the loop. Repeat to make four cradled bead charms.

6. Attach the leaf pendant to one of the simple bead charms from step 5 and attach another jump ring.

7. Attach jump rings to each of the shell beads. To make a simple shell charm, attach a second jump ring to one of the shell beads.

8. To make a dangling shell charm, string a large bead onto an eye pin. Make a loop in the eye pin and trim any excess wire. Attach the two remaining shell beads from step 7 to one of the loops. Attach a jump ring to the other loop (photo 2).

9. To make a beaded tassel charm, thread the needle with a comfortable length of thread. Fold the thread in half, tie the ends together, and tie to the loop of an eye pin.

10. String 10 size 11° seed beads onto the thread. Loop the thread around the last bead and draw it back through the previous nine beads. Draw the thread through the loop in the eye pin and secure with a knot.

11. Repeat step 11 to make five strands of beads extending from the eye pin (photo 3).

12. String the tube bead onto the eye pin. Make a loop in the eye pin and trim any excess wire. Attach a jump ring to the loop (photo 4).

13. To make a dangling heart charm, string the small heart pendants onto a jump ring. Attach a second jump ring to the first jump ring.

14. Attach eight charms, equally spaced, to one of the chains.

15. Attach the remaining charms to the other chain and connect the ends of the chains together with jump rings. To finish, attach a clasp to one end of the bracelet and a jump ring to the other end.

photo 1

photo 2

photo 3

photo 4

about the designers

Christine Calla designs jewelry for Half the Sky (www.half-the-sky.org). In addition to being an accomplished designer, Christine is the mother of three—she includes her husband in that tally. You can contact her at christine@half-the-sky.com.

Jean Campbell writes about, teaches, and designs beadwork. She has written and edited more than 45 books, including *The Art of Beaded Beads*, *Steampunk Style Jewelry,* and *Creating Glamorous Jewelry with Swarovski Elements.* Jean is a Create Your Style Crystallized Elements Ambassador for the Swarovski company and contributes to BeadingDaily.com. She is the senior editor of *Beadwork* magazine and conducts lectures and teaches jewelry-making workshops throughout the United States. Contact Jean through her website: www.jeancampbellink.com.

Marie Lee Carter began learning her craft in a metalsmithing class at the Fashion Institute of Technology in New York. She used a range of skills that allowed her to work at home without the chemicals and fumes of solder, pickle, and buffing compounds. In each of her pieces, Marie aims to tell a short story in precious metal and stone. Her website is http://mariecarter.com.

Candie Cooper is a jewelry designer who loves unique materials and color combinations inspired by her years in China. She's the author of several Lark titles: *Metalworking 101 for Beaders*, *Felted Jewelry*, and *Designer Needle Felting*. Her next release will be *Necklaceology*. Candie has also contributed to other Lark books, including *Fabulous Jewelry from Found Objects*, *Beading with Crystals*, *Beading with World Beads*, and *Beading with Charms*. Candie creates designs for craft-industry companies, publications, and on-air talent. She teaches workshops internationally and has appeared on PBS. Visit www.candiecooper.com.

Patty Cox developed nearly half of the projects included in *Dazzling Bead & Wire Crafts*. Her 25 designs for that book included jewelry, napkin rings, a picture frame, cocktail skewers, a clock, and a bookmark.

Rachel M. Dow specializes in fabricated sterling silver, metal clay, and found-object jewelry. She also makes handspun, hand-dyed yarn. Her work is shown in selected galleries and at www.rmddesigns.com.

Sherry Duquet believes that jewelry should be whimsical and expressive. "I am inspired by the brilliance of natural gemstones," she says. "When you put on a piece of jewelry, it should make you want to sing out loud." Since starting Solstice Designs with a fellow designer, Sherry has developed a loyal following. Visit her virtual store at www.solsticed.etsy.com.

Pat Evans, an artist, a teacher, and a writer based in San Jose, California, loves helping her students develop their innate creativity and teaching them the skills to bring that creativity to life in exciting designs. Her specialties are metal-clay jewelry, mixed media, and fused glass. She also likes to experiment with a wide range of media, from basket making to photography. She's an Art Clay senior instructor and a columnist with *Metal Clay Artist Magazine*. Email her at pat@patevansdesigns.com.

Diane Guelzow of A Common Thread (http://acommonthread.weebly.com) is a wife, a mom, a special education teacher, an empty nester, an art educator, and a lady who likes to keep busy. She's working toward her doctorate in education (Ed.D) at Appalachian State University in Boone, North Carolina, with a focus on expressive arts therapy. In addition, she stays involved with art making, including jewelry and book arts, and she's currently advancing her pottery skills.

Jackie Guerra became the host of the television show *Jewelry Making* after an appearance on DIY Network's *Celebrity Hobbies*, where she shared her lifelong hobby of making jewelry. Jackie also works as a comedienne, an actress, an author, a designer, and a public speaker.

Beki Haley has been beading for most of her life. Her business of selling beads and jewelry supplies has been going strong since 1985. Visit www.whimbeads.com.

Michaelanne Hall is a self-taught artist living in Asheville, North Carolina. She sells her jewelry in a gallery there.

Gary Helwig is the inventor of the WigJig family of tools and accessories and currently holds three patents for the WigJig tools. Gary works for the WigJig Company on the WigJig website, developing new jewelry-making projects. He has more than 200 copyrighted jewelry designs that are published on the WigJig website. Gary has performed many demonstrations making jewelry with wire and beads and occasionally teaches classes. He lives in San Antonio, Texas, with Suzanne, his wife, and Boomer, the family dog.

Mary Hettmansperger is a fiber and jewelry artist who has been exhibiting and teaching across the United States and abroad for 28 years. She has given her instruction and artwork to SOFA; the Bead&Button Show; national and regional fiber conferences; basketry, jewelry, and beading conferences; and more. Mary has authored, illustrated, and contributed to more than 10 Lark Jewelry titles, from *Heat, Color, Fire & Set* to *Fabulous Found Object Jewelry*. She does segments for the PBS programs *Beads Baubles and Jewels* and *Quilting Art*, and her work has been in magazines like *Art Jewelry* and *Bead&Button*. Her email is maryhetts@gmail.com, and her website is www.maryhetts.com.

Tamara Honaman is immersed in beads, wire, metal, and all things jewelry. She has been making jewelry for more than 16 years and contracts for Fire Mountain Gems and Beads as a jewelry designer and educator. She has appeared on PBS's *Beads Baubles and Jewels* and DIY Network's *Jewelry Making*. Tamara is a certified Precious Metal Clay and senior Art Clay instructor and is the founding editor of the magazine *Step by Step Beads* and three other publications.

Lilli Johnson has enjoyed a lifelong passion for jewelry. After experimenting with several forms of jewelry making, she fell in love with working with wire, specializing in designing custom links on the Delphi wire jig by WigJig. Lilli and her husband, now grandparents, live in Pennsylvania. If you have questions about the bracelet or working with wire and WigJigs, contact Lilli at lillijohnson9@hotmail.com.

Susan Lenart Kazmer is an award-winning jewelry designer who works in mixed media, found objects, and metals. Her work has been included in museum exhibits throughout the country, including the Smithsonian; The Art Institute of New York City; and the Huntington Museum of Art.

Cindy Kinerson is a self-taught bead and metal artist. She and her husband own a bead and jewelry supply shop in Reno, Nevada, where Cindy designs jewelry and teaches beading workshops. Cindy is also a metal clay and Art Clay instructor for the Nevada Art Museum. She finds inspiration in combining unlikely elements, with her latest creations involving seed beads on metal. Her designs have appeared in national magazines and books, as well as in several galleries and museums.

Nancy Kugel is an accomplished artist with a craving to learn new things, get familiar with new mediums, and explore a variety of artistic outlets, with each new foray adding a new distinction to her artistic style. Media include jewelry, sketching, needlework, sculpting, and wood carving/burning—these are just a few favorites. You can contact her at nancykugel@gmail.com.

Mami Laher is a jewelry designer and an artist who loves searching for originality and uniqueness in creative expression. She prides herself on making bead and wire jewelry with no jig—only basic tools. She enjoys painting with watercolors and has an affinity for flowers, abstract as well as real. She can also be found ice-skating. Mami originally hails from Japan but now resides in Los Angeles. View a sampling of her jewelry, glass beads, and paintings on her website www.mamibeads.com.

Elizabeth Larsen works as a biologist for Snohomish County in Washington State but started beading as a hobby in 2001. Her work has been published in beading magazines and books and can be seen on her blog: http://saichandesigns.blogspot.com.

As a mixed-media artist, **Linda Larsen** has been designing jewelry for many years. As the owner of ObjectsandElements.com, she spends a lot of time looking for treasures and developing new products for the jewelry supply website. She teaches at several national shows and blogs frequently about projects and techniques at http://objectsandelements.typepad.com.

Valérie MacCarthy got her start in jewelry design as a child. As a present, Valérie's grandmother gave her a box of beads and some string. From this humble beginning, she developed a passion for creating colorful and organic earrings, necklaces, and bracelets. Her creations have been worn on the runways of New York Fashion Week and graced the pages of high fashion magazines. In 2007, she moved to Paris and launched her jewelry collection under her own name: www.valeriemaccarthy.com. An opera singer by trade, Valérie continues to fulfill the growing demands for her jewelry while appearing on renowned stages all over the world. She is the author of *Beading with Gemstones*.

Carol McGoogan discovered quilting and the fiber arts more than 10 years ago. Since then, her creative journey has taken her to explore book arts, collage, jewelry making, and metalwork. Her work has appeared in *Cloth Paper Scissors* magazine, and she contributed to *The Adventurous Scrapbooker*.

Marlynn McNutt has been the lead jewelry designer for Fire Mountain Gems and Beads and created many of the inspirational designs featured in the company's catalogs. She has taught numerous classes for bead shops, small groups, and tours. Marlynn's work has been featured in *Simply Beads*, *Bead Unique*, and several books. She has also appeared on eight segments of the show *Beads, Baubles & Jewels* on the PBS Channel.

Kaari Meng is the owner and operator of the Hollywood-based store French General. She has designed jewelry for companies such as Anthropologie and has sold her jewelry to specialty shops around the world. She wrote the Lark Jewelry & Beading title *French-Inspired Jewelry* and *French-Inspired Home* and has been featured in *O*, *Martha Stewart Living*, and *Romantic Homes* magazines. Kaari also wrote *Home Sewn*, *Handmade Soirees*, and *Treasured Notions*. Kaari and her husband, Jon, designed a line of paper arts for EK Success. French General continues to design fabric for Moda and the quilting industry. Visit www.frenchgeneral.com.

Geri Omohundro is an award-winning stained glass artist living in the Snake River Canyon of southern Idaho. She fell in love with shaping glass in a flame during a Cindy Jenkins bead-making workshop and now creates dichroic glass beads and explores ways of showcasing them with wire-wrap techniques. See more of Geri's work at www.advancetogoartglass.com.

Tair Parnes, a Tel Aviv fashion designer, is inspired by diverse international influences. Trained in art forms ranging from weaving and working with gold to making tapestries, she travels the world learning about different techniques, styles, and color combinations. Tair is the author of *The Aspiring Artist's Studio: Beaded Jewelry*.

Erin Prais-Hintz designs jewelry in Stevens Point, Wisconsin, where she lives with her husband and children. Collaboration is key to Erin's creativity, and she enjoys nothing more than connecting with other artists and telling stories through her wearable art. Visit http://treasures-found.blogspot.com.

Wendy Remmers was raised in Hawaii by a mother who had her hands in every art and craft hobby, so it was no surprise that Wendy would develop similar passions. She studied fine arts at the University of Hawaii at Manoa, majoring in graphic design, and worked with Hawaii's top public relations agency. In 2000, Wendy decided to focus her life on her passion of beading. In 2002, Wendy and her husband Scott opened Brea Bead Works, in Brea, California, where Wendy teaches beadweaving, metalworking, soldering, metal clay, and chainmaille. Visit her website at www.breabeadworks.com.

Rachel Sims is a world-traveling, book-devouring, street-treasure-finding, Rhode Island School of Design educated glass artist and silversmith with a penchant for quirky design. She left designing luxury watches in Switzerland to move back to Iowa to create jewelry and teach workshops. Her work can be seen at http://fuzzishu.etsy.com, and a full list of classes can be found at www.fuzzishu.com.

Andrea L. Stern grew up surrounded by artists, so she knew one day she'd make some kind of art. She started with drawings and then moved on to painting, beadwork, and quilting. You can find samples of her work at http://andreasternart.blogspot.com and www.embellishmentcafe.com.

Marty Stevens-Heebner is the founder and president of the Rebagz Handbags line. Her designs have appeared in dozens of magazines, including the cover of *WWD/ Women's Wear Daily*, as well as on *The Today Show*. She has appeared on HGTV and the DIY Network and is the author of *Altered Shoes: A Step-by-Step Guide to Making Your Footwear Fabulous*. You can see her handbags at www.rebagz.com and contact her at marty@rebagz.com.

Terry Taylor was an author and editor for Lark Books for 15 years. His books include *The Altered Object, Chain Mail Jewelry, Artful Paper Dolls*, and *Altered Art*. His undeniable masterpiece, however, was undoubtedly the smash best-seller *'Stache*, which released to great acclaim. In his new life, he's studying jewelry in the Professional Crafts Program at Haywood Community College in Clyde, North Carolina.

Barbara Van Buskirk is a freelance graphic designer and bead artist. A transplanted New Yorker, she lives in Asheville, North Carolina, with her extraordinarily tolerant husband and daughter. Barbara lives by the motto, "You can never have too many beads!" She can be reached by email at barbaravb@pipeline.com.

Wendy Witchner is constantly on the road traveling to shows, while living and working out of a motor home. She shows three lines of jewelry that include wire and mixed metal. The limitations of life on the road, with minimal tools, has led her to use primarily cold connections and wire. She incorporates an eclectic mix of materials into her designs, including crystals, bali silver, pearls, and antique buttons from the late 1800s.

Hanni Yothers grew up on Lake Huron in Michigan's beautiful Upper Peninsula. When she discovered stones and metal and realized that these pieces of the earth could be made into beautiful jewelry, her career path was set. She has been selling her jewelry in fine shops and galleries for almost 20 years and is represented in several national catalogs. Hanni lives in northern Michigan with her husband, their daughter, three golden retrievers, and assorted animals. View her jewelry at www.heyjewelry.com and www.facebook.com/hannigallery.

index

project index

If you already know your favorite materials or processes, use this list to find projects made using specific types of beads or techniques.

acknowledgments

Many thanks to Hannah Doyle, who put in the hours to help pull this book together and refine its rough edges. Without our art directors' hard work and flair for lovely layouts, this book wouldn't be nearly as elegant and organized. And of course, the deepest thanks and appreciation to the designers who shared their jewelry for this book, which owes its dazzling imagery and accessible approach to their masterful skills.

about the author

Nathalie Mornu works as an editor for Lark Jewelry & Beading. She studied metals and wood for five years at the Appalachian Center for Craft in Smithville, Tennessee, and has dabbled in many crafts over the years, so as a sideline she sometimes creates projects for Lark publications—stuff as varied as stitched potholders, beaded jewelry, a reupholstered mid-century chair, a weird scarecrow made from cutlery, and a gingerbread igloo.

Nathalie's author credits include *Chains Chain Chains*, *500 Felt Objects*, *Quilt It with Wool*, and the best-selling *A Is for Apron*. For the recent jewelry book *Leather Jewelry*, she learned on the fly and made a handful of projects. Since discovering leather as a craft material, Nathalie continues to design jewelry, and she's been slowly teaching herself to make sandals. She's filled with regret for all the years she could have spent building a hoard of breathtaking skins and creating magic with them.

When it comes to bracelets, Nathalie has a recommendation: for best results, wear a whole mess of them all at once!